Fort Wayne Cityscapes

Photo Research by Lynne Shuman

"Partners in Progress" by Sharon D. Little

Produced in cooperation with the Allen County-Fort Wayne Historical Society

Fort Wayne Cityscapes

Highlights of a Community's History

MICHAEL C. HAWFIELD

Dedication:
For my wife, Diana, who was a creative force in all that she touched.

Windsor Publications, Inc.—History Books Division
Vice-President/Publishing: Hal Silverman
Editorial Director: Teri Davis Greenberg
Director, Corporate Biographies: Karen Story
Design Director: Alexander D'Anca

Staff for *Fort Wayne Cityscapes*
Developmental Editor: Jerry Mosher
Manuscript Editor: Amy Adelstein
Photo Editor: Lynne Ferguson Chapman
Assistant Director, Corporate Biographies: Phyllis Gray
Editor, Corporate Biographies: Judith L. Hunter
Production Editor, Corporate Biographies: Thelma Fleischer
Senior Proofreader: Susan J. Muhler
Editorial Assistants: Didier Beauvoir, Kim Kievman, Michael Nug-
    wynne, Kathy B. Peyser, Pat Pittman, Theresa J. Solis
Sales Representative, Corporate Biographies: John Swedberg
Layout Artist, Corporate Biographies: Mari Catherine
    Preimesberger

Designer: Christina Rosepapa

Library of Congress Cataloging-in-Publication Data
Hawfield, Michael C.
Fort Wayne Cityscapes.
Bibliography: p. 124
Includes index.
Fort Wayne (Ind.)—History. 2. Fort Wayne
(Ind.)—Description—Views. 3. Fort Wayne (Ind.)—Industries.
I. Title.
F534.F7H38   1988   977.2'74   88-5581
ISBN: 0-89781-244-1

The author wishes to thank the Fort Wayne
News-Sentinel *for publishing a series of articles*
which was the forerunner for this volume.

*Previous page: The searchlight cupola of the
Lincoln National Bank stands guard over the
sleeping city of Fort Wayne. Photo by Dan
Nichols*

*Facing page: Lady Liberty, a 13 1/2-foot
copper statue, is a weather vane which sits
atop the goldleaf dome of the current Allen
County courthouse. Photo by Brian Gillett*

Contents

Introduction

Fort Wayne's neighborhoods have been critical to the dynamic growth and unique identity of the community from its earliest days. In these neighborhoods, formed around business, government, and religious centers, the people who came to settle in Fort Wayne found that curious mixture of mutual support and stimulating competition that lies at the heart of any healthy city environment.

Fort Wayne began as an assembly of Miami Indian villages, which they called Kiskakon, or Kekionga, meaning "The Blackberry Patch." Even then, before Europeans entered the scene, the region that became known as Fort Wayne was a crossroads. The St. Mary's River and the St. Joseph River meet to form the Maumee River; it is the short distance, of about nine miles, between the confluence of these rivers and the headwaters of the Wabash River, known as the Maumee-Wabash Portage, that gives the area of Fort Wayne its great importance. The great Miami war chief, Little Turtle, said it best when negotiating peace with General "Mad Anthony" Wayne in 1795, at the end of the Indian wars. For Little Turtle and his people the Three Rivers was "that glorious gate . . . through which all the good words of our chiefs had to pass from north to south and from east to west." From this point a traveler could follow the St. Mary's into the heart of Ohio, or up the St. Joseph River into Michigan, or down the Maumee to the eastern Great Lakes. More significantly, a traveler could cross the Portage to the headwaters of the Wabash River, which led directly to the heart of the continent in the Mississippi Valley. The Midwest's natural highways thus converge on what was to become Fort Wayne. Whoever controlled such a crossroads controlled a key point in the wilderness of North America. In later years, long after the wilderness had been tamed, corporations and major business concerns would be drawn to this crossroads in the heartland of America's industrial marketplace. In the neighborhoods, around the "cityscapes" of Fort Wayne, endure signs of this lively heritage, heralding as well a dynamic present and promising future. There are churches exemplifying extraordinary organizing ability and profound spirituality; these were foundations which helped stabilize the pioneers of the frontier settlements, as well as later generations bombarded with the myriad pressures of an industrialized society. Here, too, in the neighborhoods are found the parks that provide the means for vital recreation and reacquaintance with our roots in nature. Noble or eccentric monuments, the remnants of an ancient water supply system, restored buildings—all serve as constant reminders of our origins and our ongoing challenges. Fort Wayne's history reflects nearly every facet of the rich American experience, of which these essays can only touch the surface.

Fort Wayne's Lakeside Park is a popular location for winter sports. Photo by Dan Nichols

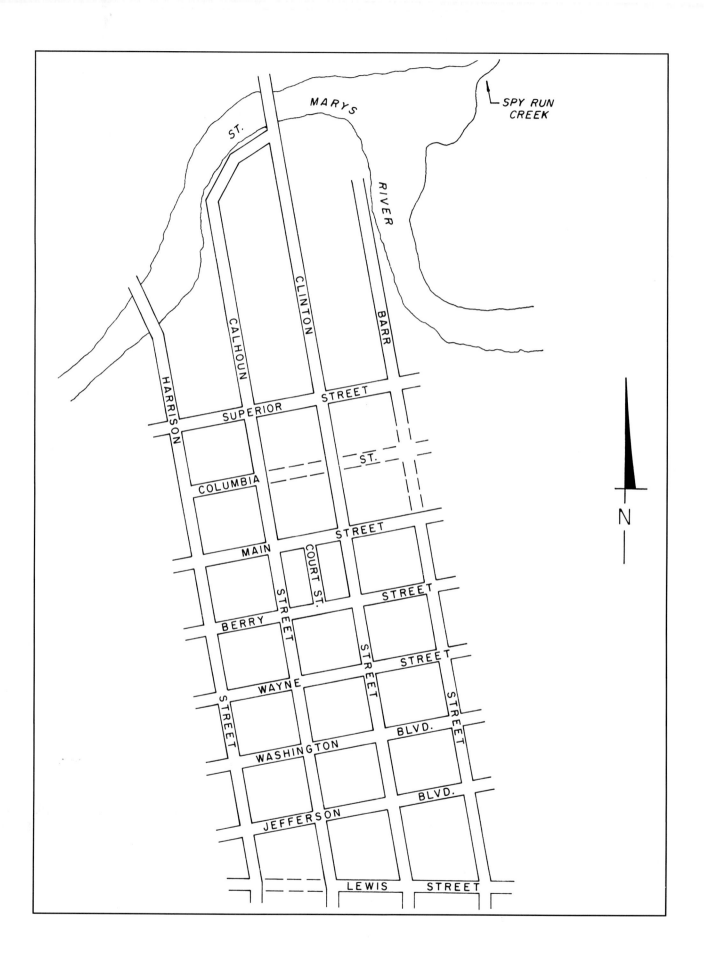

Chapter One

The Original Plat

ALLEN COUNTY'S MASTERPIECE

The best-known building in Allen County, and certainly the most unique, is its courthouse. It is also one of the finest county courthouses in the United States.

Dedicated on September 23, 1902, five years after its cornerstone was laid, the proud building cost more than $800,000. The courthouse is constructed of Vermont granite and blue limestone from Bedford, Indiana, in a balanced combination of styles from Grecian and Roman to the Renaissance. The simple Doric lines of the first floor rise to the more elaborate Ionic columns of the second story, while the ornate Corinthian and Roman Imperial styles dominate the third level. Above all is the great golden dome on which alights the copper statue of the goddess of liberty, 225 feet above the street. A wind vane, the 13.5-foot goddess invariably holds her torch of enlightenment toward the breeze.

The courthouse, 134 feet wide and 270 feet long, takes up the entire block bounded by Main, Court, Berry, and Calhoun streets. This was the

FORT WAYNE CITYSCAPES

In 1987 Fort Wayne reinstated trolly transportation, in tribute to a romantic bygone era. Each of three trolley replicas is mounted on an 18-seat bus chassis. The trolleys travel a regular downtown route and are also available for charter. Here one of the trolleys passes by the courthouse. Photo by Dan Nichols

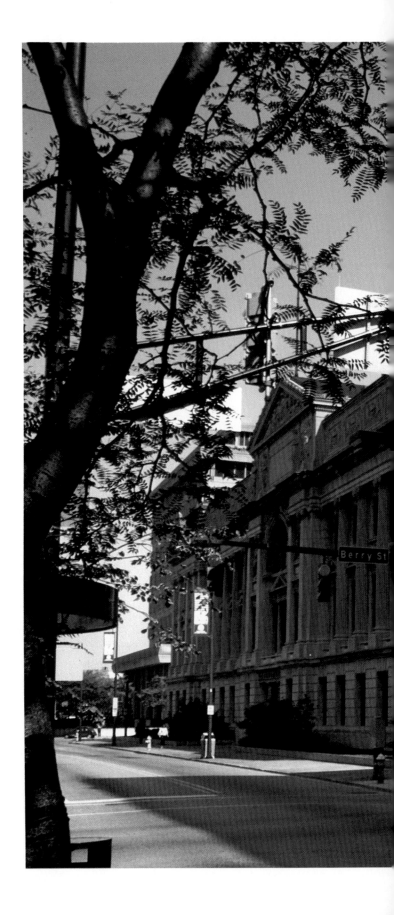

THE ORIGINAL PLAT

The present Allen County courthouse fills the entire plot originally designated as Courthouse Square, save for the sidewalk border. Its boundaries are Main Street, Calhoun Street, Berry Street, and Court Street. Photo by Bill Christie

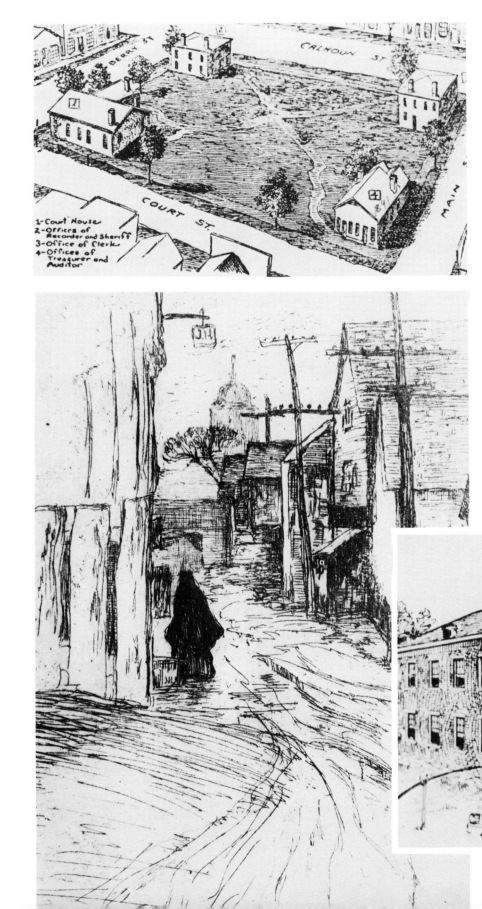

Left: An ample site for containing a city court-house was established in the original Fort Wayne plat. However, the courthouse build-ings grew progressively larger through the decades. From Griswold, The Pictorial History of Fort Wayne, 1917. Courtesy, Allen County-Fort Wayne Historical Society

Below left: This view of the courthouse from the south was sketched before 1890 by Jesse Hamilton, one of several accomplished Hamilton women. Courtesy, Allen County-Fort Wayne Historical Society

Below: Allen County's first courthouse was a modest 40 square feet. Built in 1831 at a cost of $3,321.75, it was abandoned and torn down in 1841 because of questionable con-struction. From Griswold, The Pictorial History of Fort Wayne, 1917. Courtesy, Allen County-Fort Wayne Historical Society

FORT WAYNE CITYSCAPES

The dominant buildings in the Fort Wayne skyline reflect both the city's history and its progressiveness. Photo by Dan Nichols

Built at a cost of $1.5 million, the Embassy Theatre is now estimated to be worth $16 million. To duplicate the building today would be virtually impossible, since many of the materials and techniques used, as well as the craftsmen who built it, are no longer available. Courtesy, Embassy Theatre Foundation

everything from disco and rock to a production of the Broadway musical *Irene* and a visit by Olivia De Havilland. Volunteers spent hundreds of thousands of hours scrubbing grimy floors, removing gum from seats, cleaning the grand marquis, and replacing its 15,000 light bulbs. But by the end of the first year, the Embassy Foundation was still nearly $700,000 short of the purchase price; extensions were granted and the drive went on. Students at Fairfield Junior High raised money through a special bike ride, Huntertown Elementary School held a benefit flea market, and restaurants offered a portion of their profits on each dinner sold.

Save-the-Embassy proved to be a popular fund-raiser, winning endorsements by political and community leaders. However, it remained a grassroots drive sustained by the hard work and the nickels and dimes of thousands of people. And it succeeded! By mid-1976 the Embassy had been purchased and the city council had approved its designation as a historic district, thus ensuring its survival. But several more years of fund-raising lay ahead, first to fix the roof, then to reupholster the seats, to restore the ornate plaster decorations, and most recently, to clean the building's exterior. Nevertheless, the theater is rapidly becoming part of the new Civic Center complex, as envisioned by the 1974 plans.

Construction of the Embassy was begun in 1926, and it opened on May 14, 1928, as the Fox Theatre and Hotel. This was the largest, most ornate theater Fort Wayne had ever seen. Designed by theater architect John Eberson, with the local firm of A.M. Strauss, the rococo interior was, as one enthusiast put it, "a phantasmagoric celestial environment." In the lobby the theatergoer was greeted by opulent neo-middle eastern arches, Romanesque barrel vaults with Wedgewood icing, exuberantly colored reliefs, and intricately marbled staircases, columns, and floors, all reflected in art deco mirrors and Corinthian lamps.

Left: In the last 60 years legions of patrons have been awed by the magnificent lobby of the Embassy Theatre. Courtesy, Embassy Theatre Foundation

Below: The chandeliers which hang in front of the Page organ pipe chambers at the Embassy Theatre (one on each side of the stage) are eight feet tall, weigh five hundred pounds and contain eighty bulbs. The Page organ is housed in the orchestra pit on its own base. Courtesy, Embassy Theatre Foundation

To update the experience for the twentieth century customer, advertisements for the opening of the Embassy proclaimed the theater to be "cool as a mountain top—refreshing as a seashore," for it was the only air-conditioned theater in town. Opening night, the 60-cent admission price entitled you to a special film attraction *Easy Come, Easy Go* with Richard Dix, accompanied by the theater orchestra led by Wilber Pickett. Percy Robbins played the Page organ.

Shortly after the opening, the owner of the theater, Clyde Quimby, changed the name to the Emboyd Theatre, in memory of his mother, Emma Boyd. The great electrical sign spelling out "Emboyd" was the largest anywhere in the state.

Quimby had come to Fort Wayne after World War I and quickly realized the growing popularity of film. He married Helen Kinkade, the piano player for silent movies at the Jefferson Theatre. By the 1930s Quimby owned the greatest movie houses in Fort Wayne: the Emboyd, the Paramount, the Jefferson, and the Palace (which was the debut stage for the Broadway hit *Helzapoppin'*. On one occasion, in the "gangster years" of the thirties, the excitement on the screen was played out at the box office. While Edward G. Robinson's film *Little Caesar* was premiering inside, a gunman pulled an automatic pistol on the manager, forced him and six others to face the wall, and made off with the night's receipts of $2,000.

The Philharmonic, under Igor Buketoff, frequently played at the Emboyd and continued there when the name was changed in 1952 to the Embassy. Although the orchestra no longer performed at the Embassy when the theater faced bankruptcy in 1969, its return in 1975 substantially boosted efforts to save the building.

The Embassy is heir to a theater tradition in Fort Wayne that reaches back 131 years. In 1853 the first theater in Fort Wayne, the Colerick Opera House, was opened between Clinton and Barr on the north side of Columbia Street with a performance given by the Kekionga Minstrels. The Colerick was also the first fully equipped theater in Indiana. But for a decade, use of the theater remained sporadic, presenting only occasional touring shows. The first professional company to visit Fort Wayne was the Sanford's New Orleans Opera Troupe in 1855, and in 1856 P.T. Barnum treated the town to an appearance of his celebrated attrac-

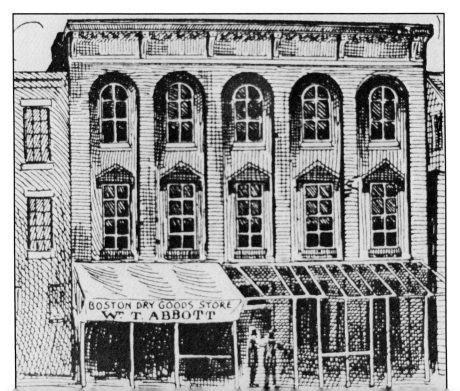

Colerick Opera House was the center of amusement in Fort Wayne. Its doors opened on the evening of December 26, 1853, and for 20 years it provided entertainment to the citizens of Fort Wayne. Noted musicians, actors, politicians, and lecturers appeared on its platform. Courtesy, Allen County-Fort Wayne Historical Society

tion, "Tom Thumb."

After the Civil War, theater interest, if not taste, improved in Fort Wayne, and the place came to have the reputation of a "good theater town." Well-known figures of the age, such as Edwin Forrest, Laura Keene, and Edwin Booth, came to the Opera House as well as the new Hamilton Theatre, a small second-story hall built in 1863 on a site approximately where today's Fort Wayne National Bank stands. The most common shows were the minstrel troupes and burlesque, with occasional productions of perennial favorites: *Uncle Tom's Cabin, The Black Crook,* and *The Hidden Hand.*

By and large, in the 1870s the local newspaper had scant praise for these productions. Critics reveled in sharp attacks on the players in much the same spirit as the audience itself, which was quick to voice complaints about whatever (or whomever) it disliked in a play.

The *Daily News* critic sometimes stooped to personal attacks on performers, as when he complained about the appearance of Olive Logan in *Amy's Experience*: "When Olive doffs her wig she also doffs her hair; she is the ugliest creature out of fairy books. If Olive Logan is uglier off the stage than she is on it, we never want to see her again anyhow."

Many productions that enjoyed popularity were wildly risque. A cancan troupe that had been run out of Bloomington was assured a sellout in Fort Wayne. In 1877 M'lle D'Est's Parisian Blondes appeared, as did the *Living Art Pictures,* which included such tableaux as the "Red Stocking Minstrels," "Female Wrestlers," and "Lady Bathers." The *News* noted that one dancer fell into the footlights but escaped burning because she had nothing on that could catch fire.

Later in the century, in the 1880s and 1890s, theater in Fort Wayne improved greatly, fortunately at the same time it expanded its season. Each year between 1884 and 1888, there were an almost unbelievable 450 presentations of 150 plays and variety shows—at a time when no performing was allowed on Sundays and when few theaters operated in the heat of summer.

After it opened on East Berry Street in 1870 for roller skating, the Rink also became a favorite playhouse. By 1880 it had been converted to a theater and renamed the Academy (also called the People's Theatre). In its heyday, companies like the

Through the good years and the lean, Fort Wayne has supported theater. Traveling troupes from New York and London sparred and parried with the rowdy frontier audiences in a succession of theater houses. The present Performing Arts Center, home of the Fort Wayne Civic Theater, is just one block from the historic site of the Colerick Opera House. Courtesy, Allen County-Fort Wayne Historical Society

The New Palace Theatre featured vaudeville acts when it first opened to the public. Courtesy, Allen County-Fort Wayne Historical Society

London Theatre Company and the American Opera Company made regular stops at the Academy, as did the Buffalo Bill/Calamity Jane extravaganza. During this time the custom arose of singing the National Anthem at the close of each play.

Other theaters, like the Broadway Theatre, the Library Hall, the Metropolitan Variety Hall, the Tivoli Garden, and the Atlantic Garden Variety Hall, were enjoying great popularity. Competing intensely with each other were other great houses such as the Olympic (later the Bijou), the Masonic Temple, the Grand Opera House, and the Majestic.

The old adage that the early theaters were great fire hazards proved true. Although Fort Wayne was spared the horror of the Iroquois Theater fire in Chicago in 1903 in which 588 persons died, all the great nineteenth-century theaters in town were eventually destroyed by fire.

The golden age of theater in Fort Wayne came in the early twentieth century. In one year alone, 1913, seven new theaters opened. The Masonic Temple Theatre was the queen of them all, and hosted such performers as Lilly Langtry, George

M. Cohan, and the Barrymores, while entertainers like Mark Twain, Eddie Foy, and Annie Oakley also made appearances. Frank James, brother of the outlaw Jesse James, appeared at the theater in *Across the Desert* in 1901. Classic plays, such as *Richard III, Othello,* and the newest works from Gilbert and Sullivan, were produced, along with such forgettable dramas as *The Mummy and the Hummingbird, Beside the Bonnie Briar Bush,* and *Whoop-De-Doo,* starring Lillian Russell.

The coming of film made little immediate impact on the theaters. Most houses, like the Majestic and the new Empress (1913), still offered mostly stage shows, though these were limited to vaudeville. Film, in any case, was only a filler. By the twenties, however, film took over the main role in the grand theaters. Into this period was the Embassy born, ornate and magical in the old style, yet up-to-date with a varied program of stage and film productions.

FIRST PROFESSIONAL BASEBALL

For nearly a half century, from 1883 to 1930, at the Jail Flats between Calhoun and Clinton streets just south of the St. Mary's River, was situated League Park, the baseball stadium that was the central sports attraction in Fort Wayne—itself the home of numerous landmarks in baseball history. Where the grandstands once stood is now the site of Poinsatte Motors.

Back in June 1883 in League Park the first night baseball game was held. Partly staged as a promotion by Ronald T. McDonald, the manager of the new Jenny Electric Light Company, the game was played between the local Fort Wayne Methodist College team and the Quincy (Illinois) "Professionals." The event took place under the brilliance of 27 arc lights that had been mounted by Jenny Electric on the fences around the field. Twice the lights went out, abruptly plunging the place into almost total darkness, but this hardly detracted from the thrilling novelty of it all. Although everyone in the overflow crowd agreed that more lights were needed and that the heavy shadows were a problem (no doubt the very reason so many errors resulted in the home team's 19 to 11 loss), the excitement stirred by the advent of nighttime baseball received more national attention on the news wires than any sporting event to date.

Flushed with such success, the owners built a grandstand in 1884, and for the next 45 years League Park hosted major league teams like the New York Yankees and the Chicago White Stockings, along with a World Series game, the beginnings of the American League, and some of the liveliest minor league and semiprofessional baseball in the country.

But baseball's beginnings in Fort Wayne preceded League Park by more than two decades. Even before the Civil War, local baseball games were common in the city. A year after the war started, on April 23, 1862, the Summit City Baseball Club was formed by Thomas Shoaff and Charles Brackenridge, with such players as Henry Olds (later an area manufacturing magnate), Charles McCulloch (son of the future Secretary of the U.S. Treasury) and Washington Haskell (the first person in Fort Wayne to ride a bicycle, among other things). Fur trader and pioneer businessman Allen Hamilton donated a portion of his land at the southwest corner of Lewis and Calhoun streets for the first organized playing field.

Enlistment in the Civil War disrupted club membership. Although some members died in the fighting, Summit City was reorganized in 1866. A new club, the Kekiongas, also was organized that year, and in 1867 other teams, known as the Twightwees, the Mechanics, the Socials, the Concordia Empires, and the Keystones, were formed. Local games were vigorously played, occasionally breaking into fistfights.

As a fledgling team the Kekiongas did not always do well. In 1869 the Cincinnati Red Stockings beat them 86 to 8. But by the end of that summer the Kekiongas' pitching had so much improved that Cincinnati in a second game scored only 41 runs to Fort Wayne's 7. When Charles Dawson, later to become judge of the Allen County Superior Court, became the club president in 1870, the team's fortunes improved. In that year the old Camp Allen site off the West Main Street Bridge, where Civil War recruits gathered before going off to southern campaigns, was converted into a baseball diamond. Before long a grandstand was added, its heavily ornamented central section named the Grand Duchess. The Kekiongas owed their boost to the disbanding of Baltimore's baseball team in the middle of its tour in the Midwest. Many of the best players came to Fort Wayne in 1870, among them pitcher Bobby Mathews, who might have invented the curve ball. The Kekiongas went on tour that summer, winning everywhere they played. So outraged were the Chicago White Stockings fans at one of their losses that they stoned the Fort Wayne team's carriage, injuring many of the players. This was the year that Fort Wayne won the state championship (and a good deal of prize money).

In 1871 the first professional baseball league, the National League, was organized in New York, and among the nine teams that paid their $10 membership fee was the Fort Wayne Kekiongas. A coin was tossed to determine the teams for the first league game, and the lot fell to Fort Wayne to host the Cleveland Forest Citys.

The event took place on May 4, 1871, and, needless to say, it was a game full of firsts. Fort Wayne beat Cleveland 2 to 0, a score that for four years stood as the lowest of any baseball game. Pitched by Bobby Mathews, this was also the first shutout. Indeed, just about every record was set. As the newspapers described it, the first pitch was a ball, but the Cleveland batter, "Deacon" White, hit a double (the first) on the next pitch, only to be tagged out in a Fort Wayne unassisted double-play (the first, of course). Bill Lennon, the catcher,

Pearl Zane Grey, a member of the Orange (New Jersey) Athletics, was one of Fort Wayne's most famous early baseball players. He later became a noted novelist. Grey is pictured in the middle row at the far right. Courtesy, Allen County-Fort Wayne Historical Society

dropped a third-strike pitch, allowing the batter to get on base (another first), but he redeemed himself later by scoring the winning run. In the end, the game was rained out.

The Kekiongas disbanded in midseason, their franchise bought by a Brooklyn club called the Dodgers. This was the last major league team fielded by Fort Wayne. Nevertheless, the succeeding years in minor league baseball were exciting. Early in the 1880s Fort Wayne joined the newly formed Northwestern League, and it was this group that became, in 1900, the other major league baseball organization, the American League.

Once the Fort Wayne team moved to League Park in 1883, numerous of its players became famous early major league stars. The most noteworthy player to join the Fort Wayne team in the early 1890s was a graduate fresh from the

Left: In the spring of 1913 League Park, located at the north end of Calhoun Street, was under water. Spring training and tryouts were held at the Concordia College gym and the adjacent playing field. Courtesy, Bob Parker

Below: In this circa 1920 photo, the Fort Wayne baseball team catches the trolley after lunching at the Hotel Kindler. Courtesy, Allen County-Fort Wayne Historical Society

University of Pennsylvania, Pearl Zane Grey. The handsome 21-year-old outfielder was a big hitter for Fort Wayne. "He was famous for hitting home runs just when necessary," one newspaper commented. But he soon moved on to play for the Orange (N.J.) Athletics. A native of Zanesville, Ohio (named for his pioneer ancestors), Grey had trained as a dentist and, after opening an office in New York in 1897, he turned his hand to writing. Despite frequent rejection by publishers, Grey finally met a Colonel "Buffalo" Jones who encouraged him in his writing of adventure tales. By 1912 Grey had gained a wide popular readership with his *Last of the Plainsmen*. Grey became one of the most successful American novelists by the time he died in 1939, having published 85 novels about the West which sold more than 100 million copies.

Effective organization of the minor leagues did not come until after the turn of the century, and in 1900 the Fort Wayne club became the leading team in the Central League, one of the best in the country. Under the leadership of players like "Bumpus" Jones, Charlie Babb, and Cy Swain, the Fort Wayne team won the league championship in 1903.

In 1908 the club was reorganized and given the name Billikens (though it is not known why). Under the extraordinary promoter Louis Heilbroner, a 4-foot 8-inch enthusiast known for his almost comically pronounced German accent, the Billikens won several league pennants and national prominence. Running the team along with Heilbroner was M. Stanley Robison, the founder of Fort Wayne's immensely popular amusement park, and the Fort Wayne *Gazette*'s sports reporter, Ford Frick, who later became one of baseball's most influential and powerful commissioners. The Billikens were a colorful lot, rich in the stuff of early baseball legend. "Shag" Shaughnessy was the manager, while "Doc" Casey (another wayward dentist) played an animated game at third base, and "Bunny" Fabrique gave his own sort of class

to shortstop, which later made him a heroic "bum" in Brooklyn. The last season for the Billikens was in 1917. In the decade before 1928, various semipro teams dominated the Fort Wayne baseball circuit, usually sponsored by local corporations. The Lincoln Lifes were led by "Bubbles" Hargrave and "Pinky" Hargrave (who later played for the Washington Senators). "Butch" Henline and Bruno Betze ably assisted "Bubbles" and "Pinky."

Throughout the 1920s Fort Wayne teams hosted many exhibition games with the most famous big league outfits. In 1920 the Lincoln Lifes played the New York Giants as well as Connie Mack's Philadelphia Athletics. On Ralph Miller Day in 1921 everyone was delighted as Casey Stengel of the Yankees clowned his way through playing centerfield. In 1924 the Fort Wayne Chiefs were formed and they, too, hosted the major teams. In 1927 the Lifes played the Yankees in a hard-fought game that finally brought Babe Ruth, in the year of his record 60 home runs, to the plate in the tenth inning to break the tie. The first pitch was a strike that caused the Babe to grouse loudly; he swung and missed the second pitch, putting the Yankees in danger of losing. But on the third pitch the great home run king hit the ball out of the park. According to the Bambino himself, it was the longest home run he ever hit, because the ball landed on a freight train that was passing the park at that time. This was the last year for the Lincoln Lifes.

The Fort Wayne Chiefs dominated area baseball for the next decade. At one point they were the farm team for the St. Louis Cardinals. But this was also the era when the old League Park was destroyed. In 1930 the stadium, which had withstood even the great flood of 1913, was apparently the victim of an arsonist. Police theorized that an irate fan, possibly the one whom stadium officials struggled with over two baseballs he had caught during a game and refused to give up, came back to the park at night and set the place afire.

Whatever the cause, the stadium was not rebuilt. Yet, in later years, semiprofessional men's baseball, women's professional baseball, and boys' baseball made their mark in national sports history. The semipro G.E. Voltmen won the national championship in 1946 through 1949, and the new Kekiongas of the Fort Wayne Civic Baseball Association won both national and world titles. The Daisies were one of the finest teams of a unique women's baseball league that caught the local imagination from 1945 to 1954, and which produced such heroines as Dottie Collins, Donna Cook, and Dottie Schroeder. The Wildcat League, founded by Central Soya president Dale McMillen, is still one of the nation's most innovative baseball programs for youngsters.

All this rich tradition inspired by a national pastime is rooted in the old field along Calhoun called League Park.

In the summer of 1930, an arsonist set fire to the grandstand at League Park, burning it to the ground. Because Fort Wayne had a team that was contending for the league championship that year, the grandstand was rapidly rebuilt. Courtesy, Bob Parker

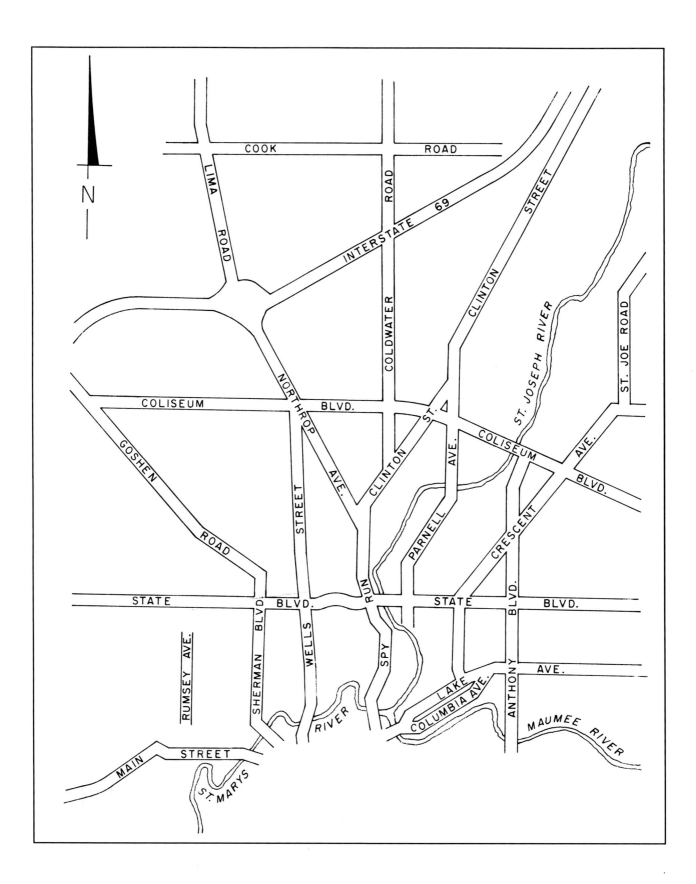

Chapter Two

The North Side

SUMMIT CITY

Today it is an undistinguished spot at the intersection of Rumsey and Wheeler streets, just west of the Norfolk & Western and the Penn Central railroad tracks crossing Fort Wayne's west side. But this intersection marks the place where, more than a century and a half ago, the great Wabash and Erie Canal began. This was the summit of the canal, a feature that gave rise to the nickname "Summit City" for Fort Wayne. It was here that the feeder canal which began seven miles away on the upper St. Joseph River met the main channel just before it crossed the St. Mary's River to enter Fort Wayne.

This spot is also close to the heart of the Nebraska neighborhood, one of the oldest and most colorful residential areas in the city. Indeed, the neighborhood got its name because it was located so far outside town. Before the canal was begun, a merchant named A.C. Hutzell built a store on the country road (later to become West Main Street) west of the St. Mary's River. A common joke in town was that every settler who followed

Hutzell had gone "out west—to Nebraska." Not to be outdone, Hutzell named his market the Nebraska Store, and the name Nebraska stuck for the entire neighborhood as it grew up along the canal basin.

The Wabash and Erie Canal that cut through "Nebraska" and Fort Wayne was the longest artificial waterway in America. It also formed the most ambitious part of the great scheme for internal improvements that swept the nation in the 1830s, and its presence had a profound impact on the emergence of Fort Wayne as a city. The idea of a canal connecting Lake Erie to the Ohio River Valley via the old portage area of the Maumee and Wabash rivers had been first suggested by George Washington in the 1790s. Similar recommendations were made time and again from 1800 to 1820, but no action was taken until 1823 when Fort Wayne pioneer Samuel Hanna and David Burr of Jackson County began to agitate in the Indiana legislature for a canal. The almost complete lack of usable roads or rivers navigable by heavy craft each year worsened the problem of getting bulk produce out and raw materials and goods into the growing community of Fort Wayne and surrounding areas.

Finally, in 1824, the state authorized the first surveys to be made, and by 1827 the U.S. government had granted Indiana every alternate section of land along the proposed route, or about 3,200 acres. The sale of these lands, it was hoped, would pay for the canal's development. A land office was opened in 1832 under the direction of the Fort Wayne Indian agent Samuel Lewis, a relative of Meriwether Lewis, of Lewis and Clark fame. The groundbreaking for the canal project was held February 22, 1832. George Washington's birthday was chosen as the date because he was considered America's foremost promoter of canals, and Fort Wayne was chosen as the site because it marked the geographical summit of the canal. A celebration was planned for the then-tiny community of about 300 inhabitants. A military band of two musicians led an enthusiastic parade to Main Street from Courthouse Square to the juncture of the feeder and main canals. The three canal commissioners marched proudly behind the band, followed by the president and secretary of the parade committee, the national color guard, and the general citizenry. Charles Ewing gave the address, which was punctuated by the ceremonious digging of the first chunks of earth. Other worthies then dug their respective spadefuls, and the parade concluded that night with the float of an illuminated canal boat built by Louis Peltier.

The first part of the project involved the construction of the feeder canal, which was laid out to run from near present-day Shoaff Park to the main canal's summit. This auxiliary canal was necessary to bring sufficient water to the main channel at its highest point. The feeder was begun in 1832 with the construction of a large dam on the St. Joseph River. Constructed of forest trees, sand, boulders, and gravel, the dam was 17 feet high and spanned 230 feet across the river. The feeder canal itself was dug along the length of the western bank of the St. Joseph River (the trench can be seen clearly today in Johnny Appleseed Park), and was taken west across the Bloomingdale neighborhood to the end of Rumsey Street. When the feeder canal was finished in 1834, the, according to the *Sentinel*, "indefatigable F.P. Tinkham" built a special flatboat for the first canal ride. As the *Sentinel* went on to report, the "entire population" boarded Tinkham's raft and poled themselves the seven miles up the feeder to the dam, where they "spent the day— Fourth of July—drinking and making merry."

The summit of the canal, 198 feet above the level of Lake Erie, or 790 feet above sea level, was also the apex of the great geological depression, or trough, formed in the last ice age. This apex marks the continental divide between the rivers that eventually run to the Atlantic, such as the Maumee and those, like the Wabash, that empty into the Gulf of Mexico. The summit was a feature that intrigued

Left: Fort Wayne's own James McBride used some imagination in making this sketch of canal commerce in the mid-1800s. Courtesy, Allen County-Fort Wayne Historical Society

Below: General Lewis Cass was the guest of honor and chief speaker at the opening celebration for the main section of the Wabash and Erie Canal. Born in Exeter, New Hampshire, in 1782, Cass was influential in the development of the Midwest. From Griswold, The Pictorial History of Fort Wayne, *1917. Courtesy, Allen County-Fort Wayne Historical Society*

the Republican newspaper in town. On March 8, 1853, the editor of the *Times,* John W. Dawson, would say he was tired of "the hackneyed and worn-out name by which Fort Wayne was christened," and suggested the place be called Summit City in honor of its altitude on the canal.

In 1832 Jesse Lynch Williams was named chief engineer of the canal. Born in 1807 near Danbury, North Carolina, Williams was the grandson of Judge John Lynch, the founder of Lynchburg, Virginia, and originator of "Lynch Law," which arose out of the judge's summary treatment of Tories during the Revolution. Jesse Williams' successes with the Wabash and Erie Canal led quickly to his appointment in 1834 as chief engineer of the entire Indiana canal system and, in 1837, as engineer of all of Indiana's transportation byways. After the canal's heyday, Williams was one of those instrumental in bringing the railroad to Fort Wayne, and he was named by President Abraham Lincoln (who became a personal friend) as a director of the Union Pacific Railroad. It was Jesse Williams who engineered the eastern linkup of the first

transcontinental railroad at Ogden, Utah.

The construction of the main canal was a huge undertaking. Building a ditch averaging 50 feet wide and 6 feet deep, with several feeder canals and locks for raising and lowering the boats to different levels of the canal path, required extraordinary labor. Work was grueling—and sometimes deadly. Disease and accidents claimed an estimated one life for every six feet of canal dug in the 452 miles from Toledo to Evansville. The "Jigger Boss" worked the rows of laborers, who were mostly Irish and German immigrants paid $10 to $13 per month, with barrels of whiskey "to ward off fever and protect from snakebite," and it was up to the workers how many jiggers of whiskey they consumed. One Jigger Boss, when asked if the men were drunk all the time, replied, "You wouldn't expect them to work on the canal if they were sober, would you?"

Conflict among the workers sometimes disrupted the project and endangered the men and their families. In 1835 the so-called Irish War erupted in the LaGro area of the canal. Irish immigrants, many from Cork in southern Ireland and a smaller number from the Ulster areas of northern Ireland, increasingly harassed one another until one faction armed itself, took up "battle lines," and awaited the attack of the other. Before matters came to blows, however, the various area militia were called in.

The Fort Wayne to Flint Springs (present-day Huntington) leg opened and began earning money in 1835. In celebration, another parade, this time led by 33 costumed ladies representing the states of the Union, preceded the launching by Captain

Captured at the Battle of Lake Erie during the War of 1812, this six-pound British naval cannon was used at the ceremony celebrating the opening of the Wabash and Erie Canal. The cannon is currently displayed in front of Historic Fort Wayne's visitor center. Photo by Lynne Shuman

Asa Fairfield of the first canal boat, the *Indiana*. Fairfield then was host to all the notables of Fort Wayne for a grand excursion on the waterway through the wilderness countryside. One observer noted there was "dancing on board and drinking good whiskey—even getting funny." Afterwards, a ball was held in the tavern of Zenas Henderson at the northeast corner of Calhoun and Columbia. By 1838 the way to Logansport was opened, and the land sales boom went into full gear. Despite the financial panic of 1837 and the gross overextension of state credit to finance the canal, optimism ran high.

In 1834, on the Fourth of July, another celebration was held to commemorate the opening of the entire canal from Lake Erie to Lafayette. Notables from across the nation sent their greetings, and the splendid Toledo Guards stood in fine military array in the mud of Columbia Street. Presidential candidate and War of 1812 hero General Lewis Cass was the guest of honor. At sunrise a cannon from the War of 1812—the same one that today stands before the visitor center of Historic Fort Wayne—was fired to start the celebrations.

Taverns and inns were filled, and the canal boats were tied as many as three deep to the town docks—all were festooned with ribbons and flags for the celebration. After some stirring band music, Cass emerged from a canal boat and stepped out onto the gangplank to hear poetry especially written for the occasion. Listening intently, according to one newspaper account, to "poetry he could not understand," Cass missed his step and fell into the canal. The portly general was whisked off to dry at the home of Allen Hamilton, one of the organizers of Allen County. Then at eleven o'clock in the morning, a huge parade formed at the courthouse square and marched to Colonel Thomas W. Swinney's homestead on the west end of town. Cass managed to give his scheduled two-hour oration, which was duly punctuated by the occasional firing of the old Lake Erie cannon. But some were convinced that the humiliation of Cass' dunking also seriously dampened his presidential prospects.

Canal travel was safe and rates were reasonable: $3.35 from Toledo to Fort Wayne. A crew of captain, helmsman, cook, and driver were typical, and on the larger boats there might also be a steward, a chambermaid, and cabin boys. Real excitement came with the debut of the showboats that could seat as many as 100 for the minstrel shows. The canal boats could be scenes of sorrow, too. In 1846 hundreds of Miami Indians were herded onto canal boats in Fort Wayne to be removed to the Ohio River and from there to new homes in Oklahoma. The chroniclers tell of the wrenching sadness in the faces of the Native Americans as they were towed from their ancient home of Kekionga.

The canal was all-important for the local economy of Fort Wayne. Although its heyday lasted only about a decade, because of the canal, inland communities like Fort Wayne were opened up to greater commerce. It wasn't unusual to see long trains of wagons filled with produce lined up at the docks in downtown Fort Wayne, waiting to load onto canal freighters.

As a financial scheme, however, the canal had failed even before it was completed. Revenues earned by canal use were greatly overestimated and never paid for more than a small fraction of the cost of the enterprise. The scandal of mismanagement plagued the canal, and bondholders pressed the state of Indiana to satisfy their claims; the state nearly went bankrupt. The coming of the railroads in the 1850s hastened the demise of the canal as it was used less and less, even for local traffic. By 1874 the Wabash and Erie Canal was abandoned, and in the next year the courts ordered that it be sold to satisfy creditors. In 1881 the Nickel Plate Railroad bought the rights to the canal, and by the mid-1880s the water was drained and the ditch filled in to accommodate the railroad tracks.

Today, the elevated course of the Norfolk &

Above: The restored canal house, facing Superior Street, is now the home of the Fort Wayne Fine Arts Foundation offices. Photo by Bill Christie

Right: Adolph Jaenicke was born on November 24, 1864, in Berlin, Germany. The son and grandson of renowned landscape gardeners, Jaenicke held a master's degree in landscape gardening from the Berlin University. He was brought to this country by the W. Atlee Burpee Company in 1889. After 20 years of success in the east, he moved to the city of Fort Wayne to become park superintendent and city forester. From Griswold, The Builders of Greater Fort Wayne, 1926. Courtesy, Allen County-Fort Wayne Historical Society

Western Railroad through the middle of Fort Wayne is the only reminder of the canal's once vibrant presence. And the spot where it all began, the canal's summit, is commemorated only by the city's popular nickname.

SULKIES AND ROSES

Lakeside Park, just off Lake Avenue, is the pride and joy of Fort Wayne's extensive park system. Its award-winning rose gardens especially are among the city's most popular features, and even enjoy a national reputation.

As early as 1930 the gardens boasted more than 350 varieties of roses in over 200 beds throughout three and one-half acres. Although more select today, with fewer varieties and less overall rose plants, the Lakeside Rose Garden remains one of the largest collections in the country.

The Lakeside Rose Garden was the special project of Adolph Jaenicke, who served as park superintendent from 1917 to 1948. A master horticulturalist and landscape designer, Jaenicke envisioned parks as something more than settings for

recreation or as memorials to veterans of past wars. He saw them also as educational centers, both for the lessons taught by nature in a living laboratory and as an introduction to the art of landscaping. In 1917 he seized upon the tremendous potential of then-new Lakeside Park, with its planned sunken garden and its romantic bridges across the langorous lakes, to give life to his dream of an extensive garden devoted to roses.

Top: First Park Board president David Foster sits at the entrance to Lakeside Park in this 1922 photograph. Courtesy, Allen County-Fort Wayne Historical Society

Lakeside Park, of course, is more than a rose garden. The park was begun in 1908 as an effort to do something constructive about the water-filled basins left by the removal of huge amounts of earth in building the riverside dikes. Residential developers, such as the Fort Wayne Land and Improvement Company and the Forest Park Company, also wanted to see those awkward flood ponds used productively, and these companies gave or sold parcels of land to the park department between 1908 and 1912. By 1912 the park department managed to make extensive improvements

Above: Adjacent to Lakeside Park is the residential area of Forest Park, with a spacious esplanade bordered on each side by beautiful homes. Courtesy, Allen County-Fort Wayne Historical Society

Born in Germany in 1863, Louis F. Curdes was 16 when he was brought to America by an older brother and settled in Fort Wayne. After working as everything from a merchant to a piano tuner, Curdes became interested in real estate in 1893. His zeal for integrity in his profession led him to join Lee Ninde in the creation of the Fort Wayne Real Estate Board in 1916, and Curdes became its first president. In 1905 the Forest Park Company was organized, with Judge William Vesey as President and Louis Curdes as Secretary. The company was created to develop a 160-acre tract bounded by Kentucky Avenue, State Boulevard, Anthony Boulevard, Lake Avenue, and Tennessee Avenue. Because of the suburban location, sales of the building lots were slow until Curdes introduced the concept of an esplanade bordered by homes. From Griswold, The Builders of Greater Fort Wayne, *1926. Courtesy, Allen County-Fort Wayne Historical Society*

to the area, spending the-then princely sum of $17,500 to develop extensive floral (not yet rose) gardens, footbridges, and the sunken garden with its concrete pavilion structures that are the hallmark of the park today. In 1916 a rustic, two-story pavilion was built for the comfort of picnickers whose numbers grew by leaps and bounds as the park was developed. By 1925 the sheer number of visitors, most of whom came by car, began to pose serious problems for the surrounding neighborhoods.

One of the most extraordinary of these nearby neighborhoods is Forest Park. With its distinctive double driveway and esplanade, or center parkway, the area is best known today for its beautiful large homes. It is a very tranquil neighborhood, with a strong neighborhood association and strict zoning regulations that prevent, for instance, opening a saloon or liquor store in the area. This was the intention of its original developer, Louis F. Curdes. Curdes, a real estate broker and builder, was part of a circle of developers and neighborhood planners in turn-of-the-century Fort Wayne, like Joel Ninde and her husband Lee J. Ninde of the Wildwood Company, who believed in the future of well-planned and regulated residential areas. They were in the forefront of such popular causes as the Clean Yards Movement and the Playground Movement, which, though seemingly trivial today, were at that time fundamental to establishing a decent living standard.

Forest Park was originally the farm of Fred and Eliza Hayden (for whom the old Hayden Park and Hayden School were named). The Fort Wayne Trotting Association leased the place from the Haydens in 1889 and established a large oval race track for trotters; this largely was the project of brewery owner Louis Centlivre's sons, who loved this form of horse racing. It was the Centlivre Company that first extended a trolley line to the trotting oval, which was then given the name Driving Park. Easily accessible to public transportation, Driving

Park was ideal as a fairground. In October 1895, when Fort Wayne launched its centennial celebration (one year late), many of the week's activities were held here. Perry Randall, a hotel owner and civic leader, had made all the arrangements, and the city and county together had agreed to pay as much as $5,000 to ensure a success. Besides other events in town, at Driving Park Governor Claude Matthews presided over several military reviews from competing neighboring towns, an "illuminated" high-wheeler bicycle parade, and a number of band contests. Mock attacks by Indians on stagecoaches and settlers' cabins (with appropriate rescues by the cavalry) rounded off the celebrations.

In 1902 the Fort Wayne Fair Association took over the old Driving Park. Some years later, in 1910, the Curtis group of stunt fliers came to Fort Wayne to put on an exhibition at the park. Their planes were shipped in by rail, carted out to the park, and there assembled to be flown—all as part of the show, of course. One of those particularly excited about the visit was a young man named Art Smith, who gained fame as Fort Wayne's Bird Boy, the city's most famous early aviator. Remarkably, Smith first saw a real airplane at this exhibition, even though he had already built and flown (not very successfully) his own vehicle. Smith was especially struck by the presence among the stunt fliers of a woman named Blanche Scott, who made world history that day when she became the first woman ever to complete a solo flight. The airplane demonstrations greatly impressed Smith, and it was at Driving Park that he later tried (again unsuccessfully) to "fly for profit," that is, to give a show sponsored by the park managers.

In 1913 Driving Park was bought by the Forest Park Company headed by Louis Curdes, who within the year converted it into the residential area that it is today.

Fred J. Hayden, prominent in the Indiana legislature and the commercial affairs of Fort Wayne, is pictured in this turn-of-the-century Finney and Lord engraving. Courtesy, Allen County-Fort Wayne Historical Society

JOHNNY APPLESEED COUNTRY

One of the best-known and certainly the most colorfully named parks in Fort Wayne is Johnny Appleseed Park. Stretching along the west bank of the St. Joseph River from Coliseum Boulevard to Parnell Avenue, it is also the park most familiar to travelers through Fort Wayne, since it is the only public campground in the city. To Fort Wayne residents, the 43-acre park is perhaps most familiar as the site of the annual Johnny Appleseed Festival. Held in September by the Old Fort Settlers Society and the parks department, this 10-year old, two-day long festival has become a fall attraction popular throughout the region.

Johnny Appleseed Park is in fact a memorial park dedicated to the memory of John Chapman,

Above: Erected to the memory of John Chapman, or Johnny Appleseed, this boulder monument stands in Swinney Park. It was dedicated in May 1916. Courtesy, Allen County-Fort Wayne Historical Society

Right: This composite was sketched in 1913 for Griswold's pictorial history of Fort Wayne. It includes images of John Chapman drawn from a woodcut, David Archer's burying ground, and an order for 150 trees. A new headstone was placed in Archer Park (now Johnny Appleseed Park) by the Optimist Club of Fort Wayne on May 25, 1935. Courtesy, Allen County-Fort Wayne Historical Society

one of America's authentic frontier heroes, who died in 1845 just outside Fort Wayne. Tradition holds that Chapman was buried in the old Archer family cemetery on the knoll that rises just above the west bank of the St. Joseph River. But most of the details of Chapman's life are shrouded in myth, and no one is certain today exactly where he is buried.

The movement to create a memorial for Chapman began in Fort Wayne as early as 1916 when the Indiana Horticulture Society raised a plaque in Swinney Park. That same year a marker was placed on the supposed site of Chapman's grave at the very top of the Archer cemetery knoll. A wrought iron fence was placed around the marker as the gift of state senator Stephen B. Fleming. A local commission was formed in 1934 to improve the memorial at the Archer graveyard, and in 1935 the Fort Wayne Optimist Club erected the stone marker that stands on the site today. But an agitator for a rival Chapman memorial site came forward with vigorous arguments that Chapman had in fact died and was buried on the eastern side of the St. Joseph River, on the farm owned by Wesley S. Roebuck, just north of the present-day Canterbury Green.

The debate centered on elaborate arguments concerning the large pioneer family of Richard Worth, friends of John Chapman. It was in the Worths' cabin that Johnny is reported to have died. The Roebuck faction had uncovered new evidence that made a forceful, if often faulty, case for his burial on the eastern side of the river. The Archer faction, in turn, produced its own new evidence. The debate became a running one-upmanship. When one side found a witness or a new document, the other side would quickly counter with its own.

The memorial commission finally decided to reject the Roebuck claims and settled on the traditional Archer site as the appropriate resting spot for Chapman's remains. Desperate, the Roebuck supporters appealed to the American Pomological Society, which after seven years of study accepted the Roebuck arguments in 1942. But the memorial commission was not swayed (nor even interested). The matter was settled when, predictably, more evidence was brought forward on the side of tradition.

The central part of Johnny Appleseed Park, a 12-acre tract including the Archer cemetery, was donated to Allen County in 1947 by William and Ruth McKay. On May 20, 1949, in an elaborate dedication ceremony—the first such event recorded on audiotape in Fort Wayne—the park was formally named the Johnny Appleseed Memorial Park and Beach. The movement to make the little park the center of a national memorial to Chapman was organized in 1956 when the National Memorial Foundation was established. Elaborate plans were laid for a setting that would include a lake, a grave shrine in a grove of apple trees, and a large visitor center that would house a museum, library, classrooms, a chapel kitchen, and custodian quarters. By the 1960s much of these plans had been abandoned, although the gravesite was landscaped and 30 acres added to the park complex.

The man to whom the park is dedicated was a legendary figure even in his own lifetime, and like his contemporaries Daniel Boone and Davy Crockett, the myths that surrounded his career stimulated the American imagination. Chapman himself was born in Leominster, Massachusetts, on September 26, 1774. Although nothing certain is known about the details of his early life, legend has it that he attended Harvard as a ministerial student. The story is told of Johnny's tragic love for a woman named Dorothy Durand; the families of the two lovers were bitter enemies. When Dorothy's family moved west Johnny followed, only to learn that she had died of a broken heart just before he found her. Years later, the legend continues, Johnny returned to plant apple blossoms over her grave.

What is clear about Chapman's early life is that he learned how to live in the wilderness and

This United States postage stamp commemorating Johnny Appleseed was issued in 1966. Courtesy, Allen County-Fort Wayne Historical Society

how to cultivate fruit trees. He was also converted to the religious beliefs of Emanuel Swendenborg, an eighteenth-century scientist and philosopher influential among intellectuals. By the 1790s Chapman was planting apple trees in western Pennsylvania. In about 1800 he moved on to Ohio, to the Licking County area in the middle of the state, always just ahead of the large-scale movement of pioneers into the region. Johnny was not alone in the apple nursery business. There were good profits to be made selling saplings to farmers trying to establish themselves on the frontier. But Chapman planted more nurseries than anyone else, and he always had an uncanny knack for choosing the most advantageous spot near the new settlements. By the 1820s he was widely known by the nickname "Appleseed."

While in Ohio, during the War of 1812, Johnny Appleseed was credited with saving many settlers from the hostile Indians allied with the British. Because he was viewed as a holy man and thus personally sacred, the Indians allowed Johnny to roam freely along the war-torn frontier, and he used this privilege to warn pioneers of impending attacks or to bring help to besieged settlements. Yet even in peacetime he never carried a weapon. Meat was repugnant to him. So careful was he not to endanger the life of any animal, one story relates, that when a hornet entered his shirt and stung him, he carefully peeled off his clothing so that the insect could escape unharmed. One Hoosier tale has it that when the gentle man noticed mosquitoes flying into his fire at night, he put out the blaze rather than be the cause of the death of another creature.

At first Johnny would beg or lease a plot of land to plant his trees. He would clear and prepare the soil, fence the area, and plant the seeds he had carefully gathered at cider presses in whichever more established settlement he had just left. But Johnny's trees and apples were never of the best quality, because he refused to improve his stock through grafting superior branches onto his

seedlings. He insisted, rather, on growing all his trees strictly from seeds. One settler in Fort Wayne described the apples as "so sour they would make a pig squeal." After 1814 Chapman began to buy land, and it is clear that he was becoming a man of considerable substance, both in real estate and in ready cash. All his money, however, was used not for personal comfort but to further his work.

Sometime before 1830, and perhaps as early as 1822, Chapman began making trips to Indiana. The first time he came to Fort Wayne was in 1834 when he bought two parcels of land along the Maumee River. One tradition has it that he came in a hollow moss-covered log in 1828 and started a nursery on the west bank of the St. Joseph River. By 1836, at any rate, he considered himself a resident of Allen County. There is no doubt that Johnny became widely known in the area, partly because of his odd dress and eccentric ways, but also because of his profound kindness.

THE ACE AND THE DAREDEVIL
Fort Wayne's airfields, Smith Field and Baer Field, were named for two of the city's leading early aviators, one a daredevil stunt pilot and the other a wartime ace.

Smith Field, located on the north side of Fort Wayne just east of Lima Road, was the city's first municipal airport, and in fact was originally called Paul Baer Field in honor of Paul Baer, the city native who was America's first ace pilot in World War I. Although attempts to establish an airport in Fort Wayne began as early as 1919, actual development of the airport began in 1925.

Close by the 156 acres of land secured for the airport by the park board, a section had already been set aside for air use as the landing field of Sweebrock Aviation, a private company formed during World War I that sold joy rides, gave flying lessons (no licenses were required then), and offered some cross-country trips. A $3 ticket would transport a passenger over the city. However,

Paul Baer was awarded the highest military honors for war service by both the American and the French governments. Among those awards were the American Distinguished Service Cross with palm, the French Legion of Honor with bronze leaf, the croix de Guerre with seven palms, the Aero Club of America medal, the Hearst medal, and the Lafayette Escadrille insignia. He also wore a Fourragere, a French shoulder cord awarded for gallantry in action. Courtesy, Allen County-Fort Wayne Historical Society

there were no paved landing strips at Sweebrock, only a relatively smooth grassy field, with the weeds regularly mowed and a carefully marked center "target." Flights, and particularly landings, were hair-raising experiences, and Sweebrock seldom had to worry about passengers demanding an additional go-round for their money.

After a sometimes difficult campaign to secure support and raise funds, Paul Baer Field (today's Smith Field) was enthusiastically dedicated in June 1925 by Mayor William Hosey before a large crowd. However, Baer himself was not there. Rather, Reverend Paul Krauss of Trinity English Lutheran Church presented a commemorative parchment to the guest of honor, French ace pilot Charles Nungesser, who then made the first official flight from the field. He was followed by Lieutenant Tourtellot in a U.S. Army Curtis, which unfortunately crashed in a ditch at the edge of the field. Later, after the crowds were gone, Baer did view the place, and commented that he felt honored to be so recognized by his hometown.

Paul Baer, the man for whom the field was named, was characterized by his father, a Fort Wayne railroad engineer, as "the most timid of his four children." Paul's sister, the elder Baer recalled, was the toughest of the lot; it was she "who got in all the fights at the Nebraska School, and made a finished job of it." Timid or not, Paul was an adventurer. He left home early to serve with General John Joseph Pershing's forces in Mexico during the rebellion of Pancho Villa in 1916.

The following year, Baer joined the famous Lafayette Escadrille to fight the Germans before America entered World War I. In daring exploits along the western front, he eventually shot down eight enemy fighters, often in dogfights in which he was greatly outnumbered. He was the first American (albeit in a French uniform) to destroy enough German planes to be given the recognition of "ace." In 1918 he himself was shot down over German lines and was held captive during the final months of the war.

Baer, like so many who suffered the horrors of the war, was a more reserved man when he returned home to a hero's welcome. Some said he had grown cynical. He always seemed reluctant to accept the accolades of the home front or to recount the details of the battles he fought. He was ill-at-ease at community functions held in his honor or else refused, as in the dedication of the Fort Wayne airport, to participate at all.

Nevertheless, still the adventurer, Baer daily risked his life in test flights for airplane developers, and worked for several South American governments to open mail routes. In 1930, flying the difficult territories of southern China and again establishing air mail routes, Baer lost his life when his plane crashed near Shanghai. Fort Wayne openly mourned his passing as he was buried in Lindenwood Cemetery.

Carrying the mail to and from Fort Wayne by air was a central feature of the old Paul Baer Field. As early as 1915 some of Fort Wayne's leading citizens were clamoring for airmail service, and as soon as the war was over they began working aggressively toward that goal. In 1918 the *Journal-Gazette* devoted its full front page to the issue, but not until the old Paul Baer Field was opened in 1925 was there any chance of instituting airmail service.

The beginnings of regular passenger service out of Fort Wayne in 1928 and the Hoover administration's active support of airmail service laid the foundation. Extensive refurbishing of the old Paul Baer Field in 1930 was undertaken to meet federal requirements: new runways and concrete taxi strips were added, as were improved lighting and drainage systems, a new hangar, and a weather service which became known as one of the finest in the Midwest.

On December 6, 1930, Fort Wayne was put on the regular Chicago to Columbus route. A committee was formed to organize the elaborate ceremonies to celebrate the first airmail flight. It was

Aviator Paul Baer is buried in Fort Wayne's Lindenwood Cemetery. Courtesy, Allen County-Fort Wayne Historical Society

Right and facing page: Though their airplanes may have looked similar, Paul Baer (right) and Art Smith (facing page) were probably as different in personality as any two men could be. Courtesy, Allen County-Fort Wayne Historical Society

hoped that Fort Wayne could break the record of 70,000 pieces of mail carried on an inaugural route; businesses were encouraged to hold back as much of their billings and advertisements as possible until the fated day. Children in schools even undertook to write letters to their grandchildren 50 years hence (that is, today!) in order to increase the bulk of the mail to 75,000 pieces. WOWO Radio jumped in to organize special programs to promote the importance of the event. Nevertheless the effort fell short, and in the end only 47,000 pieces were bagged to go out.

Meanwhile, other elaborate celebrations were planned for the day. Army pilots Jimmy Dolittle and Jimmy Hazlip were scheduled to buzz the field with various stunts; the parents of local aviation

hero Art Smith would be flown over the area; and from the air, Lieutenant George Hill, the first mail carrier, would drop a commemorative wreath over the monument to Smith in Memorial Park. First-issue postal marks, cards, and envelopes had been specially created for the occasion.

However, the weather on Saturday, the day of the events, turned out poor, and the stunts and fly-over by the Smiths were canceled. The weather got so bad that the airmail service itself had to be postponed. To everyone's humiliation, that night Fort Wayne's first "airmail" went out on the Pennsylvania Railroad. The weather was awful the next day, too, but Lieutenant Hill nevertheless managed to get up in his plane and drop the memorial wreath on Smith's monument. By the time the first

When the citizens of Fort Wayne presented Art Smith with a medal set with diamonds as a demonstration of their pride, Smith's wife Aimee, pictured above, had not fully recovered from their plane crash and could not walk. As Smith described it to a newspaper reporter,"I insisted on having Aimee there that night. We turned a taxicab into an ambulance and took her. The whole population of Fort Wayne was on the street cheering while we carried Aimee across the sidewalk. The crowd followed us into the Temple theater and cheered again. We were in a box. Aimee surrounded by pillows, and I with my crutches so pleased I did not know what to do." Courtesy, Allen County-Fort Wayne Historical Society

airmail did leave the old Paul Baer Field, on December 8, 1930, in still-poor weather, the crowds had disappeared. However, Lieutenant Hill managed without fanfare to deliver the mail to South Bend.

Just before the outbreak of World War II the army bought a site south of the city for an airfield to serve fighter aircraft. At first Fort Wayne leaders pushed to have the field named after either Anthony Wayne or Art Smith. But the army insisted that the airport be named for a military figure and it chose Paul Baer. Ironically, Paul Baer himself once commented that the one place he would never recommend for an airfield, because of its frequent fog conditions, was the south side of Fort Wayne, where Baer Field stands today. The old Paul Baer Field, the original municipal airport, was then given the name it has today, Smith Field.

Art Smith was called the Bird Boy of Fort Wayne, and in his time was proclaimed by many to be "the world's greatest stunt flyer." He certainly was a classic early aviator—self-trained, daring, foolish, heroic, and short-lived. Born in 1890 in Fort Wayne, he was raised in a house at 323 East Berry Street, the site where Civil War heroine Mother George is believed to have lived and which today is the office supply store of Shrex of Fort Wayne.

Smith recalled that he was bitten by the aviation bug at age 15 while drifting in a rowboat on Lake James with his girl friend Aimee Cour. Watching a big turkey-buzzard gliding above across the sky without moving its wings, Smith became inspired to begin home studies about flying machines. Smith's parents seem either to have been especially indulgent of their only child's desires or were keenly taken by the boy's dreams. In 1910, in order to get the money for Art to build an airship, the Smiths mortgaged their home, which they later lost. Art had never even seen a plane up close, or even talked to an aviator. Nevertheless, he built a craft entirely according to magazine descriptions and secured a 40-horsepower engine for the plane. This was the first airplane built in Fort Wayne.

In January 1911 Art Smith attempted his first flight. Rolling the plane out to Memorial Park, Smith got the machine airborne. But its controls had been fitted so tightly that the plane shot up and then nosed down and crashed violently in the snow. After five weeks in bed, recovering from injuries, Smith rebuilt the plane. Then he practiced, repaired, adjusted, and practiced some more.

Several months later Smith announced that he would fly from Fort Wayne to New Haven, Connecticut, a major cross-country trip for the time. Huge crowds gathered at the Circus Grounds (today's Jail Flats) for the epic flight. Art climbed into the driving seat only to find that he had forgotten to put gas in the tank. A hat was passed among the crowd by Smith's friends and the necessary $2.50 was collected to gas up the plane. For luck Smith put his cat, named Punk, in a bird cage strapped to the back of his seat. The lift-off was perfect, but only minutes out of town the engine went dead and Smith was forced to glide the ship down to a small field. The cat was found clinging by its claws to the top of the cage; the bottom of the cage was full of boiling water from a broken radiator hose that had killed the engine. Aimee Cour and Art's other friends following in a car helped with the repairs and soon he was off again, this time successfully.

Aimee Cour's father was not at all impressed with Smith's flying. He finally forbid his daughter to associate with the flyer after Art took her up in his plane for a five-minute flight. Art and Aimee eloped in this same plane in 1912. Unable to marry in Indiana without her father's consent, the couple flew to Hillsdale, Michigan, but not without first having to land near Huntertown to call back to Fort Wayne for a new valve for the engine. Just outside Hillsdale the engine died and Art and Aimee crash-landed. They awoke in a nearby farm house, and a local minister was recruited to wed the injured couple. It was years before Aimee's father was reconciled to the pair.

Smith's career as an aviator continued, although the pay was poor, the planes dangerous, and flying conditions almost always treacherous. What Smith called landings might better be described as crashes. Furthermore, crowds for Smith's shows were not always ideal. At times they could be more dangerous than the flying. In Muncie, for instance, Smith was scheduled for an air show in 1914. But when he saw that the landing field was full of trees he refused to fly. The spectators became so angry at Smith's refusal that they charged the plane, shouting "coward" and wielding rocks and bottles. They threatened to tear the machine apart. Shocked by the violence, Smith managed to get the plane in the air after brushing a tree, but crashed (or landed!) in another field. The Muncie newspaper declared the next day that "it was a great flight."

By 1915 Smith had been able to earn a solid reputation as a stunt flyer. The large purses for flying in shows became more common. In Fort Wayne he perfected the "loop-the-loop" stunt that gave him his widest fame, and he was credited in those years with being the originator of skywriting. The 1915 World Exposition in San Francisco was his biggest show and his enthusiastic audiences there included such luminaries as Buffalo Bill Cody and Teddy Roosevelt. In 1916 Smith had a triumphant tour of Japan where in city after city he thrilled the crowds. One Japanese boy penned Smith a letter in blood, begging the flyer to take him for a ride.

During World War I and in the early 1920s Smith served as an army flying instructor, and in 1923 he was one of the first pilots employed by the new U.S. Air Mail Service. While on a night mail run in February 1926, Smith was forced down near Montpelier, Ohio, hit a tree, and was killed. Two years later, in 1928, the Bird Boy monument was raised in Fort Wayne's Memorial Park in tribute to the city's most extraordinary early aviator.

Left: Sam Wolf, who chaired the Indiana centennial pageant in 1916, was born in Fort Wayne on January 25, 1868, the son of Abraham and Lena Wolf. The Wolf family lived at the corner of Main and Webster streets for 50 years. Sam went through the Jefferson Street grade school and two years of high school, and his first earnings were as deputy clerk of the city under Wright W. Rockhill. His father eventually got tired of his political activities and told Sam to go into business. Taking his advice, Sam started his own dry-goods business. From Griswold, The Builders of Greater Fort Wayne, *1926. Courtesy, Allen County-Fort Wayne Historical Society*

Right: Fort Wayne civil engineer Samuel Edsall was the son of Peter Edsall. He came to Fort Wayne with his mother and eight brothers and sisters in 1824. Edsall became a pioneer miller and was otherwise prominently identified with the development of Fort Wayne. In 1842 he, with William Rockhill, established the famous "stone mill," (known also as Edsall's Mill or Orff Mill) on the banks of the St. Mary's River north of Main Street at Rockhill. Courtesy, Allen County-Fort Wayne Historical Society

water system. Before 1879 the small fire detachments in Fort Wayne, bearing such names as the Anthony Wayne Company, the Hermans, and the Wide Awake, had to pump water by hand or steam engine from the canal, the rivers, or an inadequate system of fire cisterns.

The means to correct the situation was a matter of great public debate in 1879. After considerable controversy over competing plans, Fort Wayne finally adopted a system that called for a large pumping station and reservoir, to be located by North Clinton Street on Spy Run Creek. A second reservoir also was needed in the southern part of town, and in that same year, 1879, for $24,000, the city bought the 12-acre tract between Creighton and Suttenfield streets from the heirs of early Fort Wayne entrepreneur Allen Hamilton. Unlike the reservoir built at Clinton Street, the new reservoir in the seventh ward was elevated, so that no pumping machinery would be needed. Gravity alone would exert enough pressure to produce a stream in fire hydrants that would be strong enough to reach even the tallest building.

In 1880 the reservoir mound was built around a great storage tank. The excavation for the mound created a neighboring lake. Even at this early date, when little attention was paid to such things, the city's civil engineer, Samuel Edsall, had envisioned plans for a fine park, with rustic bridges, woods, flower gardens, and shrubbery. Although these elaborate plans never came to fruition, the park that did develop there was a favorite attraction for decades, well into the twentieth century.

Fort Wayne's reputation as a city of festivals had its origins in 1916 when the city celebrated Indiana's centennial. Even the Three Rivers Festival could learn a few things from this granddaddy of all civic festivals.

Billed as the greatest civic celebration in the country, the centennial celebration of Indiana's statehood spread through the heart of Fort Wayne. "Res" Park was chosen as the site of the centennial's pageant. A 14,000-seat amphitheater was built against the reservoir mound, facing the artificial lake. The stage, flanked by two huge pylons, was placed on an island built into the lake.

At the opening ceremonies for the festival, on Sunday, June 4, 1916, 600 representatives from all the churches of Fort Wayne joined on the island to harmonize in patriotic songs; among these was the first rendition of "The Fort Wayne Hymn." The next day, the huge industrial exposition opened at the northern end of Calhoun Street, showing off the products of Fort Wayne's factories.

Throughout the six-day long celebration, visitors were treated to circus acts three times a day. On June 6, Fraternal Day, a great parade of organizations took place, in which societies, clubs, and unions from all over the Midwest participated. June 8 was Woman's Day, which centered on the Woman's Building, the old Central High School, which housed a multitude of historical exhibits.

The centerpiece of the festival, however, was the historical pageant titled "The Glorious Gateway to the West." This six-act extravaganza portrayed the grand events in Fort Wayne's past, from the time of the first French forts and the expeditions of Anthony Wayne to the enlistment of the volunteers who first went off to the Civil War (several of these fellows were actually in the pageant). Sam Wolf, of Wolf & Dessauer, chaired this event in which more than 1,100 Fort Wayne citizens, young and old, a 60-piece band, and "a gorgeous dance by 140 girls" added a special personal character to the portrayal of the city's heritage. More than 14,500 people attended the opening production, and on closing night three days later, 14,000 children were admitted free.

Among the curiosities of this great festival was the debut of the official Fort Wayne flag. Designed by Guy Drewett, it was unveiled at the opening ceremonies. The flag displayed the familiar white bars on a blue background; however, its two-star design emblematized Fort Wayne as Indiana's

Reservoir Park, shown in a 1911 photograph, is used more than any other Fort Wayne park in the winter. Hundreds of children and adults enjoy skating and coasting there. Courtesy, Allen County-Fort Wayne Historical Society

second city. Hostile reaction to the "second city" idea persuaded Drewett to change the design to that used today, which depicts a fort, an Indian, a French fleur-de-lis, and a British lion.

After the gala events of 1916, the grandstands were removed and Reservoir Park returned to its quiet existence as a neighborhood recreation center. By the 1950s, the reservoir itself was no longer used and the great tank had become a public danger. In 1959 the reservoir was filled in.

Two decades later, however, Wayne Township Trustee William J. Cooper began an aggressive campaign to turn the old "Res" into a beautiful park, much as Edsall, a century earlier, had imagined it should be. A $122,000 project was launched, and by the 1975 season the lake had been cleaned, deepened, and given a new concrete wall; and on the north side a service building was built. Although there are still no rustic bridges, two lighted fountains make the park one of the most attractive in the city. Its great mound, once a part of the city's waterworks and later the foundation for one

Above: Pennsylvania Railroad locomotive 7218 was rebuilt in 1920 and retired in 1933. Courtesy, Walter Sassmannshausen Collection

Facing page: Looking east across the Wabash and Pennsylvania tracks, one could see this view of the Bass Foundry. Courtesy, Allen County-Fort Wayne Historical Society

of the largest amphitheaters in turn-of-the-century America, ensures that Reservoir Park will remain unique among Fort Wayne's many parks.

LINES WEST

The great expanse of the main post office complex between Clinton and Lafayette streets is an impressive facility. Yet not very long ago this area formed the central part of a much larger railroad operation called the Pennsy Shops. These locomotive and railroad car shops extended east nearly three miles along today's Conrail tracks, to Moeller Road on the edge of the city.

For nearly half a century, from the Civil War until just past the turn of the century, Fort Wayne was one of the most important railroad centers in the country. At one time, along the Pennsylvania line alone, 50 trains a day stopped in Fort Wayne:

this is one every half hour, and on just one of the seven railways in town. What made Fort Wayne a railroad center was the complex of shops where locomotives and cars were designed, built, tested, and repaired or overhauled. Hundreds of locomotives and thousands of railroad cars were built here. Here, too, worked the "West Enders," those railroaders who, with the brim of their caps characteristically turned up, took immense pride in pushing the great steam engines (and themselves) to maximum performance. And here labored hundreds of craftsmen, who built some of the most luxurious passenger cars in the nation. The shops themselves were the central feature of all this activity, and they were a part of the very beginnings of railroading in Fort Wayne.

Even before a train had ever been seen in Fort Wayne, in 1852 Samuel Hanna, a director of the first area railroad, donated five acres east of Clinton Street for shop grounds. The next year, in 1853, John and Charles Cooper purchased land east of Barr Street, put up some buildings (a blacksmithy, foundry, and machine shop) and organized the first railroad shop as Cooper & Company. Sion Bass, later a Civil War hero, bought into the operation in 1854, making it the Cooper, Bass, and Company Shops, but in 1857 these private interests sold out to the newly formed railroad company, the Pittsburgh, Fort Wayne & Chicago line (later the Pennsylvania Railroad). The Pittsburgh Shops, as they were then known, grew rapidly with the outbreak of the Civil War in 1861. Under full production during the war, these shops, in concert with the new Bass Foundry across the tracks, provided considerable materials for the Union armies.

After the Civil War, railways throughout the nation expanded greatly, and the demand for better engines and cars redoubled. In Fort Wayne the

Right: This Class X Pittsburgh, Fort Wayne & Chicago Railway Company engine, number 273, was designed and built in Fort Wayne. Locally it was called a "Steffin" engine, after its Fort Wayne designer. It later became a Pennsylvania Railroad Class G3. Courtesy, Allen County-Fort Wayne Historical Society

Below: Pennsylvania Railroad engine 7067, known as "Fat Annie," is shown at the Fort Wayne Shops in 1907. Note that the brand new engine has no dirt, grease, or road grime. The powerhouse smokestacks are in the background. Photo by George A. Niebel. Courtesy, Walter Sassmannshausen Collection

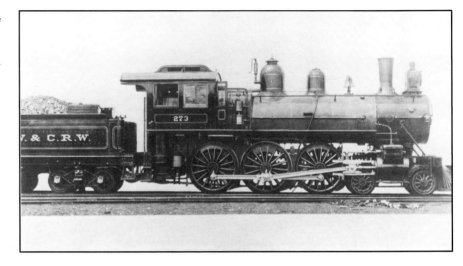

basic design of the Pullman was refined to produce the Fort Wayne Silver Place Car. This elegant sleeping car, resting on the best springs available, ensured a comfortable ride, and was carpeted inside with a rich, brilliantly colored moquette to match the velvet upholstery of its silver-armed seats. Silver ornamentation highlighted the brightly painted ceiling. The black walnut woodwork boasted gold trimmings; the lamps cradled fine cut-glass globes. An adjustable table could be set up between the seats, and mirrors could be automatically replaced by lamps with the push of a spring. Between 1867 and 1869, seven of these cars were built in Fort Wayne at a cost of $18,000 each.

Under the direction of Fort Wayne-based master mechanic James Boone, the locomotive assumed a leading position in the railroading world of the 1870s. "Boone-built" locomotives broke many performance records, frequently reaching speeds of 60 miles per hour. In 1870 railroaders everywhere were stunned to learn of the run made by Number 199 between Fort Wayne and Chicago. Engineer Anthony Wayne "Tony" Kelker pushed the passenger train to 75 miles per hour, and railroad offices throughout the country hung his picture on their walls as an example of engineering

skill and courage.

Also designed in Fort Wayne was the Pennsylvania system's superb Class X locomotive, called the Steffin Engine (after its designer). Built at the Pennsy Shops between 1892 and 1897, 28 were produced in one year alone (1895). These were high performance engines. One, for instance, although it had left Fort Wayne an hour and a half late and made all its scheduled stops, arrived in Chicago only 14 minutes behind the appointed time.

Among the Pennsy Shops' final locomotive design successes was that of the "K-2." It was patterned after the unique experimental engine called "Fat Annie," which was a huge engine, much heavier than those normally found on the flat midwestern lines.

Even as late as the 1930s, "Fat Annie" caught

The imagination of railroaders. One young fireman named Harvey Lehman, who grew up in a railroading family on Calhoun Street, built a large model of this train in 1929 while convalescing from an accident. Using the very materials used at the Pennsy Shops, including black graphite paint for the engines, Lehman fashioned "Fat Annie" with the loving attention to detail of someone familiar with the machinery. Every Christmas he set up the lighted train for his family and friends; today the model is part of the annual Christmas display in the Historical Museum.

Walter Sassmannshausen, a history teacher at Geyer Middle School, has passed on to us vivid images of working conditions in the Pennsy Shops

The roundhouse at Lafayette Street was used as a car shop at one time, but all trace of this enterprise was gone by 1930. Courtesy, Allen County-Fort Wayne Historical Society

The old Lafayette Street roundhouse is pictured between 1900 and 1905. Courtesy, Allen County-Fort Wayne Historical Society

early in this century, especially in the blacksmith areas. There, remembered one veteran, the smoke of the coke and wood furnaces was so thick that a worker could not see the person next to him. Nearly every part of the locomotive was forged there, from the bolts and rivets to the axles and frames; only the car wheels were produced elsewhere, at the nearby Bass Foundry. Work crews were set up under a foreman for eight-hour shifts. If the foreman were Irish, the crew would all be Irish; if he were German, his crew would all be German, and so on.

Fort Wayne no longer made locomotives after World War I, and much of the engine work in the Pennsy Shops turned to repair and overhauling. One of those engines overhauled was Engine Number 7002, which in 1905 had set, at 127 miles per hour, the record for American passenger speed, a record which still stands today. Old Number 7002 was refitted in Fort Wayne early in the 1920s and was to be shown off at the grand opening of the Chicago Union Station on June 23, 1925, as the special train for the Pennsy Shop Band, which toured everywhere on the system. With engineer Charlie Sommers (whose son Byron founded the Medical Protective Company) at the throttle, the refur-

bished champion set yet another local record for speed on the straight line between Fort Wayne and Chicago. This was much to the discomfort of the band members, who complained "that the wooden cars bounced, bucked, and rolled so violently that they feared the roofs would peel back."

After locomotive rebuilding in Fort Wayne ended, in 1933, the Pennsy Shops continued to produce new and rebuilt passenger cars. Nevertheless, the shops declined sharply after World War II. A few locomotives were serviced in Fort Wayne for such events as the Chicago Railroad Fair in 1948 to 1949 and for an exhibition of old engines in 1950. But the air brakes shop finally closed in 1953, and portions of the property were sold piece by piece over the next decade, until 1966, when the shops' original site along Clinton was abandoned. Finally, in 1984, the old roundhouse, perhaps the most symbolic feature of the once great Fort Wayne railroading complex, was torn down.

BLOODY RUN LANDS

The square half-mile known as South Wayne is one of the most familiar districts of Fort Wayne's south side. Once a favored hunting area of the Miami Indians, South Wayne today is a residential district characterized by a rich mixture of architectural styles and a strong sense of neighborhood unity. Indeed, almost a century ago South Wayne was, for a brief moment, a fully incorporated town separate from the city of Fort Wayne.

Geographically, South Wayne lies south of Creighton Avenue, north of Rudisill Boulevard, and west of Hoagland Avenue to the St. Mary's River. Near its center today is the sprawling modern complex of Lutheran Hospital, which is flanked by Fairfield School and South Wayne School. Prominent in the northern part is Emmaus Lutheran Church and its school. In the southern area is Packard Park, a playground, where once stood the great Packard Piano Company that closed half a century ago. Also in this southern end is the Fort Wayne Bible College, which is more than 80 years old. The names of the streets that crisscross South Wayne, such as Fairfield, Nuttman, Packard, and Wildwood, recall some of the more notable settlers and developers of Fort Wayne.

For these and other early settlers the area was a byword for good hunting, luxuriant woods, and —especially for youngsters—adventure. Exciting tales were told of the Indians who lived, hunted, and sometimes fought there. A stream that emptied into St. Mary's River just west of the old Wells Street Bridge was known as Shawnee Run. Noted for its many plum trees, it got its name from the Shawnee bands of Indians who lived along the St. Mary's in the 1820s. More luridly, this stream was also called Bloody Run. Stories tell of a Miami Indian who stabbed to death a Shawnee (or, was it an Ottawa?) on the steep banks of the creek in 1824. Enraged kinsmen of the murdered man armed themselves for revenge, and the whites in the region of Fort Wayne feared a general uprising that would endanger them as well. At this point, the stories continue, Jean Baptiste Richardville, chief of the Miamis, fortunately stepped in and mediated a settlement, convincing the wronged family to accept a retribution payment, and thus

Chief Jean Baptiste Richardville (Pechewa) was born to Joseph Drouet de Richardville, a French trader, and Tacumwah, a sister of Chief Little Turtle, in 1761. "He was," according to John Tipton, who knew him well, "the ablest of diplomats. If he had been born and educated in France, he would have been the equal of Talleyrand." Courtesy, Allen County-Fort Wayne Historical Society

averted the general bloodshed that surely would have followed.

Chief Richardville was the first owner of the lands that became South Wayne. Born in about 1761, he was the offspring of Chief Little Turtle's brilliant sister, Tacumwah, and a French trader named Joseph Drouet de Richardville. Given the Miami name Pechewa, Richardville preferred to use his French name, and he became representative of those Native Americans who adapted to the whites' culture.

A peaceful, even timid man by nature, Richardville rose to become civil chief of the Miamis, Little Turtle being their war chief. If Richardville's fame rested on his own reputation as a mediator and businessman, his success rested on the very capable shoulders of his mother. She not only engineered his rise to civil chieftain, but also managed to gain control of the lands along the ancient portage trail, which became the basis of the Richardville fortune. Richardville himself, through extensive land sales, took advantage of the great increase in pioneer immigration that followed Indiana's admission to statehood in 1816.

In exchange for supporting the American cause in the Indian treaty negotiations in 1818 at Marysville, Ohio, Richardville was given vast tracts of land south of the old fort, on both sides of the St. Mary's River. Much of South Wayne was included in this grant, but in 1828 he gave this portion back to the U.S. government, which began to sell its lots to new settlers.

Destined to be known as "the wealthiest Indian in North America," Richardville was branded by some as a hypocrite and a traitor to his people. Yet to others, like Indian agent Senator John Tipton, who had found it easy to negotiate with the accommodating chief, Richardville was "the ablest diplomat of whom I have knowledge."

Among the first investors in South Wayne was James Barnett, the partner and brother-in-law of Samuel Hanna. An amiable man, known as Uncle Jimmy, Barnett had first visited Fort Wayne in 1797, and he was with General William Henry Harrison's relief expedition when the fort was besieged by Indians in 1812. In 1818 he settled permanently in Fort Wayne and built the town's first brick house, on East Columbia Street. In 1827 Barnett and Hanna built a small dam in the St. Mary's, and downstream they erected a mill just south of the recently constructed bridge over the river. Old Mill Road was later named after this mill, and the bridge that carried the Indianapolis State Road (Broadway, today) across the river to the Little River Turnpike, or Bluffton Road, was the chief southern route out of Fort Wayne.

During the 1840s and 1850s South Wayne remained a wilderness. Game was plentiful. One old-timer remembered that pigeons roosted in such numbers in the sycamore trees along the St. Mary's that he was awakened in the middle of the night by the noise of tree limbs breaking under the weight of the birds. Wolves became such a menace that bounties were offered, and farmers competed with one another in the number of wolf traps they could set. Ague, or malaria, was common. One settler recalled that "quinine was as necessary and as regular an item as the staples of diet. Every fence was decorated with advertising notices of Ayres Ague Cure. Nevertheless, South Wayne went right on ashaking." It was not until the 1870s that the area was properly drained and the disease brought under control. Among the important developments that occurred in the district during this period, the William Barton family sold its extensive acreage to Wayne Township, and the homestead was turned into the first county poor farm, or asylum. It was used as a "pest house," or isolation ward, when a cholera epidemic struck in 1849. This deadly disease hit again in 1852 and 1854, and one doctor estimated that as many as 600 died in those three attacks.

Prosperity was such in the 1870s and 1880s that there was considerable agitation to incorporate South Wayne as an independent town. In large measure this movement began in order to prevent Fort Wayne from annexing the area for its tax revenue. The first petition for incorporation, filed in 1872, stirred a bitter court fight with the Fort Wayne city council. In the end the city failed to annex the area, but South Wayne also failed to win independence. Fifteen years later the movement for incorporation was taken up again, this time led by William J. Vessey and Henry Ninde. By 1889 the county commissioners agreed to order a general referendum of South Wayne residents to decide the issue. An overwhelming vote for incorporation was returned, and South Wayne was declared by the commissioners an independent town of Allen County.

Independence lasted until 1894. By that year the costs of sidewalks, sewers, water works, and Jenny Electric lights at the intersections had become so great that the town board was forced to levy a stiff property tax—the very thing the citizens had sought to avoid by fighting annexation by the city. Many residents thus began to see benefits to becoming part of Fort Wayne. But because the majority still voted for continued independence, the issue went to the higher state courts. Fort Wayne attorney James Barrett finally won for the city, and South Wayne was annexed in 1894.

After the turn of the century South Wayne's community centers began to assume their own identities. South Wayne School was established, and Pastor Philip Wambsganss founded the Emmaus Evangelical Lutheran Church and School. The old Wildwood estate of the Ninde family was sold to the Lutheran Hospital. On the south side of the community, again in 1904, the Fort Wayne Bible College was begun. Joseph Ramseyer and his family arrived from Kansas and bought a five-acre tract along the dusty Rudisill road. By the next year, they had dedicated the college's first building.

The pace of growth in South Wayne is best illustrated by the appearance in 1871 of the Fort Wayne Organ Company on Fairfield Avenue, where Packard Park is today. Isaac T. Packard came to South Wayne from Chicago in 1871, his organ company there having been destroyed by the "Great Fire" of October 9. Although Packard himself died only two years after establishing his new organ business in South Wayne, the company was taken over by Stephen Bond, a banker, who made the business one of the finest of its kind in the country.

The old Fort Wayne Organ Company fared well up until the Great Depression of the 1930s. After the death of Stephen Bond in 1907, his son Albert took over the business and made it a model of management-labor relations in the early twen-

The slogan of the Fort Wayne Organ Company was, "If there is no harmony in the factory, there can be none in the piano." From Griswold, *The Builders of Greater Fort Wayne, 1926. Courtesy, Allen County-Fort Wayne Historical Society*

tieth century. The name of the company had been changed to the Packard Organ Company in 1899, and, after abandoning the faltering organ business, became the Packard Piano Company in 1915. A highly productive company, it donated its skills in woodworking to the war effort in 1918 by making propellers for U.S. Army war planes. But in February 1930, scarcely four months after the Crash of 1929, the company went into receivership and finally collapsed that same year. Thus disappeared the sole industry in the primarily residential district of South Wayne.

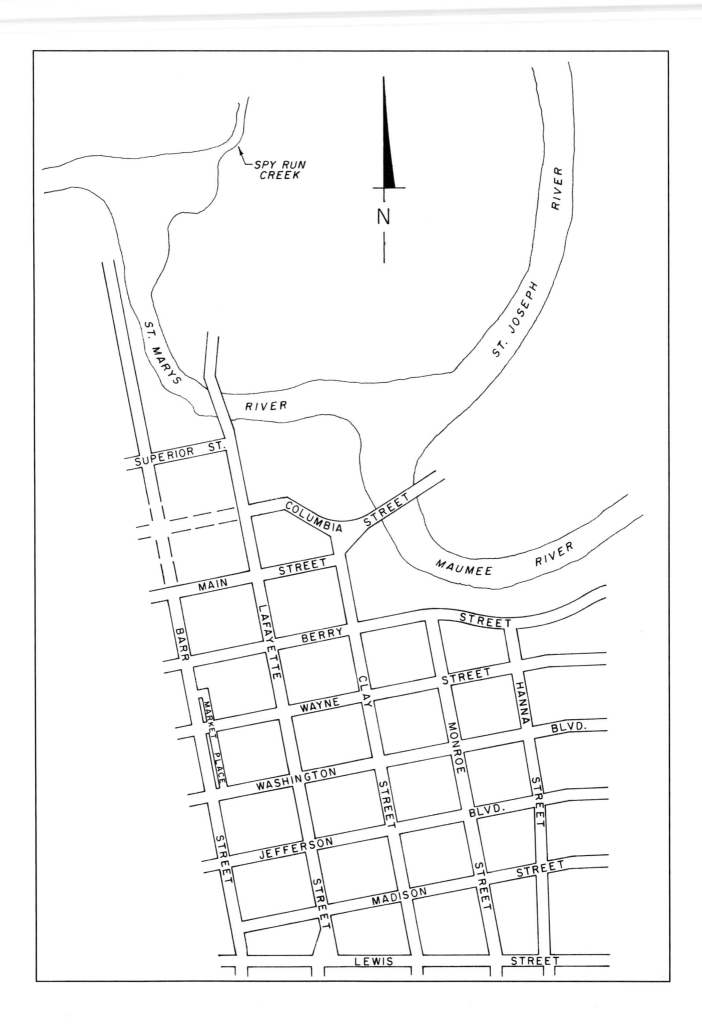

Chapter Four

The East Side

TWO GOTHIC CHURCHES

$\mathcal{T}$hroughout the United States there is no other community that enjoys as rich and vital a Lutheran heritage as that of Fort Wayne. An outstanding monument to that rich history is the oldest of the city's Lutheran churches, St. Paul's, on Barr Street.

On October 27, 1837, the Reverend Jesse Hoover, miller and entrepreneur Henry Rudisill, and 69 other Lutherans met in the second county courthouse. This building was so poorly constructed that people seriously feared it would collapse in the next brisk storm. Yet here they organized the congregation and determined to build their own church and school. This tuition-supported school was established in the basement of the Presbyterian church, then the only church building in town; and Hoover taught there with the help of two women trained in education, one of whom was Susan Mann, later the wife of Hugh McCulloch, Secretary of the Treasury under President Abraham Lincoln. But the congregation itself continued to meet in the rickety courthouse assembly room, their prayers

Above: This line drawing of the second St. Paul's church building includes the school (which had been the first church) and the parsonage. Courtesy, Allen County-Fort Wayne Historical Society

Facing page, top: A worthy successor to Pastor Hoover, Friederich Wyneken arrived in the fall of 1838. He was destined to become "the patriarch of Lutheranism on the American continent west of the Alleghenies." Wyneken, a pioneer missionary among German Lutherans throughout the west, was later a highly respected president of the Missouri Synod. Courtesy, St. Paul's Lutheran Church

made the more ardent with every strong gust of wind.

Within months after Reverend Hoover died, the Fort Wayne Lutherans attracted to their community a man who became one of the foremost Lutheran pastors in America, Friederich Wyneken. Under Pastor Wyneken the congregation began construction of its first church in September 1839. Two years later the pastor left for his native Germany, determined to recruit help for the missionary needs of the Indiana wilderness. One of the results of this visit was the recruiting of Dr. William Sihler, who was destined to succeed Wyneken at St. Paul's in 1845. Soon after Pastor Sihler came to Fort Wayne, a new church building was begun.

The most important event that took place in this second St. Paul's was the formation of the Missouri Synod, which today is one of America's largest Lutheran disciplines. In July 1846 several of

Below: Church members and neighbors gathered to hopelessly view the still-smoking devastation of St. Paul's Lutheran Church on the morning of December 3, 1903. The horse-drawn pumper was late to arrive because it was being used to put out another fire. All that was saved was the brick skeleton. Courtesy, St. Paul's Lutheran Church

the foremost Lutherans in America met at St. Paul's and adopted the first draft of the constitution of the synod. In that same year, again because of the St. Paul's connection, the Concordia Theological Seminary was transplanted from Bavaria, Germany, to Fort Wayne. Reverend Sihler immediately became one of its faculty, thus beginning a relationship between school and church that for decades remained close.

After Reverend Sihler died in 1885, his assistant, the Reverend Henry Sauer, succeeded him as the new pastor of St. Paul's. Not to be outdone by the newly erected cathedral or the newly rebuilt St. Mary's Catholic Church nearby, Dr. Sauer determined to erect a third St. Paul's; this church, or rather its basic structure, today dominates Barr Street, just south of the city market. The local architects J.F. Wing and M.S. Mahurin were retained to design the soaring Gothic church, and

Right: St. Paul's Lutheran Church is pictured during its 150th anniversary year. Courtesy, St. Paul's Lutheran Church

Facing page: In 1905, when this photograph was taken, the sanctuary of St. Paul's differed only slightly from the original design. The graceful columns and arches were a bit sturdier in the new sanctuary. A modern addition was electric bulbs in the chandeliers. Courtesy, St. Paul's Lutheran Church

$70,000 was committed to the project. On September 15, 1889, the church was dedicated. Inside, 1,500 worshipers could be seated under the great central chandelier that held nearly 200 lights. Many of the stained glass windows had been imported from Germany.

Nearly 15 years later, in December 1903, a fire started in the basement near the coal furnace. Despite the early alarm sent in by Pastor Jacob Miller, when the fire companies reached the scene the entire front and steeple were in flames and it was clear that the building was already lost. Dozens of streams of water were hosed onto the blaze, and the steam pumpers trembled and strained to produce the highest water pressure they could, but all to little effect.

The great stained glass windows fell apart when the lead frames melted, and the steeple appeared like a huge torch as flames roared out the belfry openings. The large crowd that had gathered to watch was awestruck when, as the fire reached its height, the tall gilded cross on top of the steeple began to glow, throwing a spectacular golden light on the snow-covered roofs of the surrounding

buildings. As if to signal the collapse of the great steeple, the tower bells crashed to the ground with a loud, final peal. By morning all that was left was the blackened hulk of the walls and lower tower.

Determined to restore the church to its original state, the congregation raised $55,000 for its reconstruction. Because of the great thickness of the original brick, the walls that remained were able to be repaired, and the new church was raised on the plan and foundations of the old, with only minor modifications. The project was carried out again under the direction of Wing and Mahurin, and on April 2, 1905, the new building was dedicated.

Like those of St. Paul's nearby, the great Gothic towers of St. Mary's Catholic Church, at the southeast corner of Jefferson and Lafayette streets, stand as a proud monument to the German immigrants of Fort Wayne.

The three-spired church in red brick and stone trim is an imposing building. In height (230 feet) and length (190 feet) it is larger than its mother church, the Cathedral of the Immaculate Conception in Cathedral Square, three blocks away to the west. Inside St. Mary's, 32 stained glass windows throw an ever-changing display of colored light on the fluted Gothic columns, pews, and floors of the long 66-foot high nave and the tall transcept before the altar.

Although this building recently, in 1986, celebrated its 100th anniversary, it is not the earliest Catholic church dedicated to St. Mary to occupy the site.

The first St. Mary's was dedicated on November 29, 1848. The origins of this church lay both in the inadequacy of the only Catholic church then in town—St. Augustine's, located in what later would be Cathedral Square—and in the dissatisfaction that the rapidly growing German-speaking Catholic population felt for the French- and Irish-dominated congregation at St. Augustine's. Language and cultural barriers, as among the Lu-

therans in this same period, were especially troublesome. Although religious services among Catholics were conducted in the universal age-old ecclesiastical language of Latin, the sermons, social functions, and particularly the educational mission of the parish required the use of native languages. Because of this, the German-speaking Catholics erected next to St. Augustine's a frame building for their own use, as a school and meeting hall.

In 1848, 30 German families, among whom were the Meyers, Hoevels, Jostverts, and the Voors, bought several lots on the southeast corner of Jefferson and Lafayette for $1,700. Although this seems today to be a small amount to pay for such prime land, in 1848 the purchase was so costly that

Left: The cornerstone of the new St. Mary's Catholic Church was laid on July 11, 1886. In just 17 months the Gothic red brick and sandstone structure, a superb example of the ecclesiastical architecture of its time, was completed and dedicated by Bishop Dwenger. Its 238-foot spire towers over the modest homes of the surrounding neighborhood. Courtesy, Allen County-Fort Wayne Historical Society

Below: The Right Reverend Monsignor John Oechtering was rector of St. Mary's Catholic Church and vicar-general of the diocese of Fort Wayne. Courtesy, St. Mary's Church

five of the families mortgaged their farms to meet the payment. This first German Catholic church—a brick structure that measured 64 feet by 32 feet —was completed within the year, despite an outbreak of cholera that disrupted construction.

In 1857, under the direction of a new pastor, Father Joseph Weutz, a new and much larger church was conceived. In the summer of 1858, Bishop Luers, the first bishop of the newly created diocese of Fort Wayne, laid the cornerstone. The new church, dedicated on November 2, 1859, cost the then-enormous sum of $30,000. This St. Mary's was nearly as large as the new cathedral then under construction (it would be completed in 1860), measuring 133 feet long and 66 feet wide.

For the moment, in 1859, St. Mary's was the largest church in Fort Wayne, dominating the city's skyline with its grand single steeple nearly 200 feet high. Twelve great Gothic stained glass windows, six to a side, filled the walls between the buttresses with light and seemed to make the weight of the building disappear. Inside, the high ceiling rested on slim, steeply pointed Gothic arches, and delicate stone filigree filled the lancet openings at the ends of the nave. In addition to the ornately carved wooden screens, stair rails,

The statues on the main marble altar of St. Mary's Church are of hand-carved imported wood. The altar is one of the most picturesque in the city. Courtesy, St. Mary's Church

pulpit decorations, and altar ware, a treasured sculpture was a beautiful reproduction of Michelangelo's *Pieta*.

All this was destroyed in an instant, at 1:30 in the afternoon on January 13, 1886. The steam boiler, for some unknown reason, exploded beneath the church. The shock of the blast was felt throughout the city, and St. Mary's was left a broken shell. Worst of all, the boiler-tender was killed, and a 13-year-old girl, Alberta Willard, who was walking along Lafayette Street, was crushed to death by one of the massive front doors that was blown off the building and onto the street.

The pastor at the time, the Reverend John Oechtering, energetically drew his congregation together and led the drive to rebuild the church. The old St. Mary's was completely razed, and the cornerstone for the new building was laid by Bishop Dwenger on July 11, 1886; a year and a half later,

on December 11, 1887, the bishop, attended by the prelates of Nashville and Milwaukee, dedicated the finished church. The boiler for this new building was put in a boiler house behind the church.

Father Oechtering, who led the congregation through its most trying time, was one of the most influential pastors in Fort Wayne between 1880, when he was appointed to St. Mary's, and 1927, when he returned to his family home of Risenbeck, Germany.

True to his scholarly training in Germany, Father Oechtering wrote extensive treatises on such topics as socialism, capital, and labor. But he also wrote dramas—*William Tell* and *King Saul*—in a rather stilted "classical" style typical of the turn of the century, a comedy entitled *The Living Statue,* and a farce called *The Discovery of America.* Extremely active, Oechtering was vicar-general of the diocese, president of the Catholic School Board, and, in 1905, at the peak of his career, was named domestic prelate of the Holy See by Pope Pius X. Although one of the first of the old German pastors to use English regularly in his sermons, Oechtering was also an outspoken defender of the German heritage and language. In 1917, for example, at the height of the anti-German war fever that swept America after she entered World War I, Oechtering dared the wrath of zealots by publicly denouncing those in local government calling for the removal of German language study from school curricula.

Although the formal school programs of the church ended more than a decade ago, under the leadership of the present pastor, the Reverend Thomas O'Connor, St. Mary's has become even more concerned with the needs of the surrounding underprivileged neighborhoods. On January 22, 1975, a soup kitchen was opened, and today it continues to grow as a vital function of the church. Equally important was the beginning of the Matthew 25 Health Clinic, which opened in May 1976, and the dental clinic, which opened in 1979.

St. Mary's still provides for those in special

need, in much the same way it did nearly 140 years ago when a handful of immigrants who did not speak the language of their new country needed a religious home of their own.

ORIGINAL FORT WAYNE

Each April, Historic Fort Wayne opens to begin another season of one of the finest onsite reproductions of a historical period in the United States. Enactments by costumed performers are among the most authentic to be found anywhere. One survey of living history museums called the event "the finest on the continent."

The dream of "bringing the fort back to Fort Wayne" had been around for many years before Historic Fort Wayne opened in 1976. The Allen County-Fort Wayne Historical Society had been the hub of such discussions since before World War II. More than two decades ago, in 1964, the Pi Chapter of Psi Iota Xi Sorority gave the project a

boost by awarding the Historical Society a grant to pursue research about the three American forts built in Fort Wayne between 1794 and 1816. While this research was being carried out by Lynn Wallick and Mrs. Chris Crampton with the help of well-known Historical Society figures like Doris Perry and David Drury, the means for securing the funding and the land for the project began to materialize. Historic Fort Wayne was incorporated in 1968, and under the guidance of such community leaders as Lynn Koehlinger, Keith Barker, and Charles Walker, a six-year fund-raising program was launched to raise the $750,000 believed necessary to build the fort.

Just west of the confluence of the Three Rivers and the ancient site of Indian villages, across the St. Mary's River from the actual location of the American forts, reconstruction of the Old Fort began in June 1975. Under the direction of Brian Dunnigan, a master military historian and expert

Armed with experience in rebuilding historic sites in Mackinac and Cooperstown, New York, military historian Brian Dunnigan painstakingly prepared for the re-creation of 1816 Fort Wayne. He walked the construction site daily, supervised the character research, and planned the training programs for the townspeople who would become the soldiers, the traders, and the Indians. Courtesy, Allen County-Fort Wayne Historical Society

Right: By March of 1976 numbered logs were being shaped into Major John Whistler's fort. Although not on its original site, Whistler's fort was reconstructed on historic ground. In 1816 this four-acre plot of land was part of Wellsington, the only privately owned land in the midst of military and Indian territory; William Wells, first Indian agent, was given the tract in appreciation for his service to the United States government. Courtesy, Allen County-Fort Wayne Historical Society

Below right: The official groundbreaking ceremony for the reconstructed fort was November 19, 1974. The foundations were poured in December. Because the contractors had to learn a whole new approach to construction and the huge timbers had to be shipped from New York, the actual assembly did not begin until August 1975. Courtesy, Allen County-Fort Wayne Historical Society

in outdoor museums, the fort began to take shape at almost the same pace as the original.

Rebuilding an early nineteenth-century fort, which in many ways was a simple, straightforward structure, proved, however, to be a demanding task. Long-forgotten skills like timber shaping, log fitting, peg joining, and shingle reaving had to be learned. Even materials had to be found elsewhere. Huge oak logs were brought in from upstate New York, and were shaped and fitted according to the painstakingly researched original specifications laid out by Major John Whistler in 1815. The effort demanded of the reconstruction crew, even using powered machinery, gave a new appreciation for the accomplishments of the soldiers who had raised those monstrous timbers two stories high, shaping and fitting them with nothing more than felling axe, broad axe, and adz.

On June 5, 1976, a month before the U.S. bicentennial, the Old Fort opened amid speech making, flag raisings, and cannon firings. In keeping with the spirit of the fort, parades of drum and fife

corps, artillery units, and infantry, authenticated from the years of the French and Indian War (the 1760s) through the War of 1812, heralded the rebirth of the wilderness garrison that gave the modern community its name. Nearly 200 years ago a similar ceremony had opened the first American fort built at the Three Rivers, and had heralded its new name in honor of its founder, General Anthony Wayne.

Forts had formed a part of the Three Rivers landscape almost since the first Europeans began to use the portage between the St. Mary's and the

As early as the 1600s the French came into the region of the three rivers to deal in furs and trade goods. Being adaptable, many of the Frenchmen married Indian women and later became intermediaries between the Indians and the Americans. Those early settlers must have looked similar to these interpreters in period dress at Historic Fort Wayne. Courtesy, Allen County-Fort Wayne Historical Society

Above left: In 1791 Major General Arthur St. Clair was sent by President Washington on a campaign against the allied tribes of the Northwest. He had explicit instructions to establish a chain of forts, with the confluence of the three rivers as the central stronghold. However, St. Clair was defeated by Little Turtle on the "bloodiest battlefield of American pioneer history." This portrait of the general is after the pencil sketch by Colonel John Trumbull. From Griswold, The Pictorial History of Fort Wayne, *1917. Courtesy, Allen County-Fort Wayne Historical Society*

Above right: The defeats of General Josiah Harmar, commander-in-chief of the armies of the United States, threw the entire West into a state of alarm. Courtesy, Allen County-Fort Wayne Historical Society

Wabash rivers. Early in the eighteenth century, in 1721, a fortified post called Fort Miami was built by the French along the St. Mary's near today's Van Buren Street Bridge. After this fort was destroyed by local Indians in 1747, the French built a new fort on the St. Joseph River (near the Tennessee Avenue Bridge), just north of the several Indian villages at the confluence of the rivers. The British captured this fort in 1760, yet failed to hold it effectively after Chief Pontiac's uprising in 1763. Although the portage and the Indian nations living here figured significantly in the western campaigns of the American Revolution, the fort was never occupied by the victorious young nation.

British interest in the Three Rivers area centered on inciting violence on the American frontier by taking advantage of the native population's growing concern about pioneer incursions into the Ohio and Indiana territories. In an attempt to put an end to attacks against frontier settlements and to intimidate the Indians, President George Washington sent one army after another into the heartland of the Miamis. Led by Chief Little Turtle, first General Josiah Harmar's army and then General Arthur St. Clair's unruly forces were destroyed by the Miami and Shawnee nations. In retaliation Washington sent the Revolutionary War hero General "Mad" Anthony Wayne into the frontier. Bankrupt and slightly tainted by his scandalous separation from his wife Polly and his affair with Philadelphia socialite Mary Vining, Anthony Wayne was nonetheless a solid and aggressive leader of troops. A stern disciplinarian, Wayne rigorously trained his troops at Fort Washington (Cincinnati, Ohio), took his "legion" to Miami territory, and soundly beat the Indians, first at the site of St. Clair's defeat at Fort Recovery, Ohio, and then at Fallen Timbers, near present-day Toledo, Ohio.

Among Wayne's Kentucky troops, it is interesting to note, was Lieutenant William Clark, the younger brother of George Rogers Clark, the

Above: The 1816 flag which flies above the fort has 15 stars and 15 stripes. In 1818, when there were 20 states, Congress decided the flag should bear a stripe for each of the 13 original colonies and a star for every state. Photo by Brian Gillett

Previous page: General Anthony Wayne was a strict disciplinarian, an astute strategist, and a bold military leader. The Indians named him "the chief who never sleeps." Wayne's victory at the Battle of Fallen Timbers in 1794 was the turning point in the fight against the Indians for control of the Northwest Territory. In 1794 Wayne built the first American fort at the confluence of three rivers. This statue of the general stands today in the city of Fort Wayne. Photo by Brian Gillett

Above left: The fort, designed by Major John Whistler, was the forerunner of the western Indian fighting forts of the 1860s. Two block-houses, placed at diagonal corners, were sufficient to guard the garrison. Photo by Dan Nichols

Below left: An 1816 sentinel at the fort faces the future. Photo by Dan Nichols

Known as "The City of Churches," Fort Wayne is graced with 284 churches, cathedrals, and synagogues. Photos by Dan Nichols

The first Catholic church in Fort Wayne, the Cathedral of the Immaculate Conception stands on its original site. The cathedral was built lovingly, if hastily, by its congregation in 1834. In 1837 the original building was replaced by a more solid frame structure. The present cathedral, with 13-story spires on either side of the western portal, was dedicated in December 1860. Photo by Brian Gillett

Above: At the turn of the century every Fort Wayne neighborhood had a park and a church within walking distance. Photo by Dan Nichols

Right: In the winter, while the gardens gather strength for the next blooming season, Lakeside Park comes alive with skaters, joggers, snow fort builders, and seasonal sculptors. Photo by Dan Nichols

Left: Fort Wayne's skyline is dominated by the imposing structure 1 Summit Square. The 26-story building houses the corporate offices of Indiana and Michigan Electric Company, Summit Bank, several smaller firms, and the Window Garden Restaurant. Photo by Dan Nichols

Below left: This cast-iron column, once the cornerstone of the world's largest manufacturer of roller equipment for trains, is now a structural part of the Downtown restaurant building on the Landing. Photo by Dan Nichols

Below right: Crossings by David Black graces the front lawn of the Fort Wayne Museum of Art. Fort Wayne has been a center for the arts since the days of the Colerick Opera House; today it is home to six community organizations for the performing arts, six museums, three not-for-profit art galleries plus numerous private galleries, a symphony, a community band, and numerous choral and instrumental ensembles. Photo by Dan Nichols

In spite of its hustle, bustle, and progressiveness, the city of Fort Wayne is still surrounded by the quiet strength of families working the fertile farmland. Photo by Dan Nichols

frontier hero of the American Revolution. On this expedition Clark met Meriwether Lewis, and 10 years later Lewis and Clark teamed up for one of America's best-known exploratory expeditions into the western frontier.

After Fallen Timbers, in September 1794, General Wayne moved his army to the central Miami village of Kekionga at the Three Rivers, the present Lakeside district. Across the river Wayne chose the site to build the first American fort in the area. This fort was located at today's intersection of Clay and East Berry streets, on the northwest corner. Building began in September 1794 under the direction of a young lieutenant named John Whistler, while dragoons burned all the nearby Indian villages.

The partially finished fort was officially entered on October 21, 1794, and Wayne handed command over to Colonel John Hamtramck. On the next day, October 22, in accordance with General Wayne's plans, Colonel Hamtramck called together a parade of the garrison, fired 15 rounds of cannon, and formally announced that the new fort was to be called Fort Wayne. It was four years to the day that General Harmar's army had been destroyed by Little Turtle's warriors at a site within view of the new fort.

John Francis Hamtramck, the man who named Fort Wayne, although a valued officer, nevertheless failed to gain the full recognition of his superiors. The highest promotions did not come to Hamtramck partly, it seems, because of his looks; President Washington himself noted that he was not at all impressed with Hamtramck's short, stocky features. Only five feet, five inches tall, Hamtramck was once likened to "a frog on horseback," and Washington thought that "a man of more dignified character should be employed." But Hamtramck was clearly a capable soldier. Born in Quebec in 1756 of Luxembourg parents, Hamtramck distinguished himself in the Revolutionary War. The commander of Fort Pitt and builder-commander of Fort Knox and Fort Steuben, Hamtramck was also a stern officer. Once Hamtramck noted that a man caught deserting his post "wouldn't talk until I cut him twice."

Hamtramck's command at Fort Wayne, given in recognition of his bravery at the Battle of Fallen Timbers, was a troubled one. The six companies left at Fort Wayne in the winter of 1794 to 1795 suffered greatly from cold, hunger, and desperate boredom. Supplies dwindled and livestock was stolen. Cavalry horses died at the rate of three each day. Hamtramck complained that "I have flogged soldiers until I am tired. The economical allowance of 100 lashes, allowed by the government, does not appear a sufficient inducement for a rascal to act the part of an honest man." But these problems plagued every frontier garrison.

In the end Hamtramck was given command of Detroit in 1796, and then, in 1801, of the Department of the Lakes, a major district. He died suddenly in 1803 at the age of 47, and was mourned by the people of Detroit, where he was well liked.

By 1798, only four years after the first had been constructed, a second American fort was begun on a different site and under the command of Colonel Thomas Hunt. It was during Hunt's tour of duty at the fort that his wife bore the first white child born in Fort Wayne. Not completed until 1800, the fort was built a short distance north of Wayne's original fort. Again, the young engineer John Whistler directed the construction.

This fort withstood the assault of the Indian wars that erupted between 1800 and 1812. These wars were provoked by encroachments on Indian lands, the disintegration of native culture, and the goading of the British. During these years the first Indian agency, under William Wells, was opened, and Quakers sought to instruct the tribes of the Three Rivers in farming techniques. But also at this time William Henry Harrison successfully pressured the Indians into ceding more of their land to the U.S. government, and the illegal

A Miami Indian woman displaying her 1816 trade goods on the floor inside her cattail wigwam is portrayed by an interpreter at Historic Fort Wayne. Courtesy, Allen County-Fort Wayne Historical Society

whiskey trade wrought tremendous damage among the tribes.

In reaction, Tecumseh and his mystically inclined brother known as the Prophet campaigned among the Indians of the region to resist land cession and white cultural influence. Both Indian leaders visited Fort Wayne in 1807 and 1808, when Captain Nathan Heald was commandant. But both Heald and Indian agent Wells had done much to relieve the suffering of hundreds of Indians who had come, forced by hunger, to the fort, and thus helped weaken the influence of Tecumseh and the Prophet among the Miamis and Potawatomis gathered near Fort Wayne.

When war did finally break out, with the Battle of Tippecanoe in 1811 (near Lafayette, Indiana, today) against Tecumseh, and in the next year against the British and their Indian allies, forts all along the frontier were attacked.

Fort Wayne, now held by only 100 men com-

manded by Captain James Rhea, came under siege by 1,000 Indians. But the attacks were repulsed after about a month by the arrival of a rescue force led by William Henry Harrison, and the war moved further north to the area around Detroit where, finally, Tecumseh and the British were defeated.

While the war raged around Lake Erie, command of Fort Wayne was given to Major John Whistler, the officer who many years before had seen to the building of the first two American forts. When Whistler arrived in 1813 he found the place "very sickly," with only one officer fit for duty and the fort itself in great disrepair. Determined to improve the fort by redesigning it, Whistler proceeded, building by building, to replace the old with new structures.

The overall design for this new fort, completed in 1816, was the most sophisticated of any yet to appear on the frontier. Indeed, Fort Wayne became the model for many military forts as the

Left: Since Major Whistler allowed only four Indians inside the fort at a given time, it was common for them to gather outside the walls and conduct their business with the Indian agent. In this reenactment at Historic Fort Wayne, the Miami and Potawatomi meet with Benjamin Franklin Stickney, the third Indian agent for the U.S. government at Fort Wayne. Courtesy, Allen County-Fort Wayne Historical Society

Below: On the site of the last American fort, at East Main and Clay streets, stands the Old Fort Well, a reminder of the simple inception of the city. Photo by Brian Gillett

frontier pushed further west.

THE HAPSBURG HORROR

It was called by some the Hapsburg Horror when city officials, led by Mayor Charles Zollinger, moved into their new headquarters at Barr and Berry streets in the spring of 1893.

But the Old City Hall, as it later came to be called, won praise from the press and city officials when it was dedicated early in the evening of April 20, 1893. The *Gazette* said it was "an ornament to the city ... a triumph of the genius, toil, persistence and ability" of the architects. The reporter was referring to Fort Wayne designers J.F. Wing and M.S. Mahurin, who were by then widely known in the state as architects of schools, churches, homes, and municipal buildings in the style of Henry Hobson Richardson, the foremost American architect of his day. Another reporter at the dedication was so transported by the occasion that he proclaimed the building "the most elegant appearing and most economically constructed city hall in Indiana or anywhere else."

Not everyone shared that opinion. The Hapsburg Horror tag, besides being a political gibe at the mayor's German ancestry, alluded to the sizable tax levy of over $60,000 imposed to build it—a royal figure for those times (royal as in Hapsburg, the German royal house that ruled Austria at that time).

Before the Old City Hall opened, Fort Wayne really had no functioning city hall. In the years just after 1840, when Fort Wayne was incorporated as a city, official business was conducted in various locations scattered throughout the Court Street area. Only the plot of land donated by Samuel Hanna, at Barr and Berry streets, had actually been set aside for the city's public business; but here, in 1855, the Barr Street Market was built.

Frustrated by the inconvenience and disorder this arrangement caused the city bureaucracy, the city council ordered in 1869 that a new market building be constructed, and that offices in this building be provided for the city clerk and the city treasurer. This was the first step toward centralizing the municipal government. By the next year, business had increased so much that the council ordered these offices "be fixed up, but not extravagantly." The city lawmakers even went so far as to provide that gaslight illumination in the offices

be supplied through the city's franchise with the Fort Wayne Gas Company.

Yet despite all the improvements to this first municipal building, by the 1880s the great increase in population and the expansion of developed land in the city made the need for more suitable facilities clear. It was the dream of Charles F. Muhler, mayor from 1885 to 1889, that the city undertake a building project which would result in one of the largest city halls in Indiana. A committee headed by the mayor and formed in 1885 convinced the city council to approve a tax levy over the next several years to provide the funds for this project. These levies provided almost $69,000 for the building fund. But it was in Mayor Zollinger's administration that the project was actually brought to completion. The old market building was destroyed and, complete with new furnishings, the new City Building, as it was officially named, was finished in 1893 at a cost of $69,806. Although later generations often scorned the soot-stained fortress-like city hall, in the eyes of many contemporaries the structure was magnificent. Its very bulk conveyed the image of power and authority citizens could admire and re-

The Barr Street Market, as seen in this 1893 photograph, was a central feature of Fort Wayne as a growing trade and industrial settlement. The brick market house was later razed to provide space for Fort Wayne's first city hall. Courtesy, Allen County-Fort Wayne Historical Society

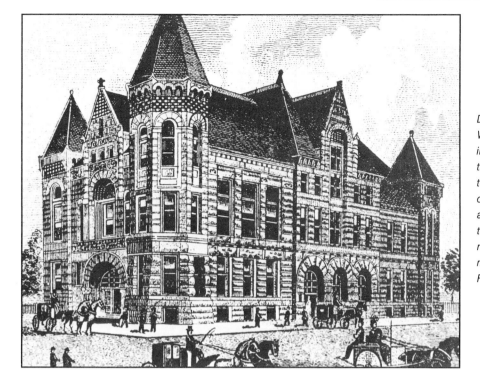

Designed by Wing and Mahurin, leading Fort Wayne architects, the first city hall was built in 1893 at a cost of over $69,000. In 1971 the city government moved into new quarters on Main Street. By the end of that decade the stone fortress had been reopened as the home of the Allen County-Fort Wayne Historical Museum. What was once the real jail now exists as a permanent exhibit and a reminder of times past. Courtesy, Allen County-Fort Wayne Historical Society

Distinguished by its onion tower, this two-story structure was built to serve as a market house and town hall. Courtesy, Allen County-Fort Wayne Historical Society

spect. Integral to this imposing image was the building's rear portal, which led to the dank basement jail where society's offenders and ne'er-do-wells were conspicuously taken.

By the mid-twentieth century the city had once again outgrown its office quarters, and in 1971 the Old City Hall was abandoned. City officials moved into the new and equally imposing quarters of the City-County Building on Main Street. Meanwhile, the all-too-familiar debate over the fate of an old building—in this case, Old City Hall—went on. Many wanted to see the Hapsburg Horror razed. Others, however, sought to preserve the structure and turn it over to some productive use. By the late 1970s the building's fate was decided, and in a great united fund-raising effort by the Allen County-Fort Wayne Historical Society, the city administration, and numerous individual and corporate donors, the Old City Hall underwent a $1 million renovation to become the second largest museum of its kind in Indiana. This museum houses tens of thousands of artifacts and operates an exhibition facility unlike any other in the state. Large temporary exhibitions now fill the 3,500 square feet of the municipal courtroom, and the permanent galleries won the 1982 American Association for State and Local History's national award for excellence in portraying local history.

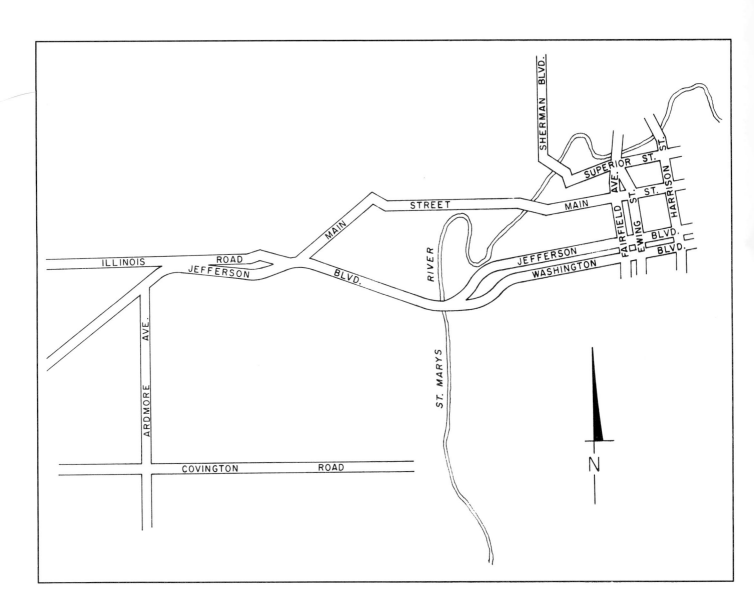

Chapter Five

The West Side

DOWNTOWN'S OLDEST BUILDING

*T*he oldest building in central Fort Wayne is the Edsall House, now located on the southwest corner of Main and Webster streets. Built in 1839 by William S. Edsall, it is also the last surviving example of the Federal style of architecture in the downtown portion of the city.

The survival of the building as it stands today is closely linked to the beginnings of ARCH, Fort Wayne's volunteer architectural preservation organization. Having successfully worked to save the Canal House on Superior Street in the years just before the U.S. bicentennial celebrations , preservationists formed ARCH as a united effort to maintain historically significant buildings, realizing that these are a community resource all too easily ignored. The Edsall House, standing on a block slated for demolition in a redevelopment project, was chosen as ARCH's pilot project. The extensive research ARCH carried out persuaded the Fort Wayne Redevelopment Commission to support the preservation of the Edsall House as a significant part of the design scheme for the entire area.

Just 90 years after the death of William Edsall, the Home Builders Association Board of Directors approved a recommendation by the Building Search Committee to lease/purchase the Edsall House, accurately and tastefully restoring it to house the association's offices. Photo by Dan Nichols

The excellent exterior renovation of the building was carried out by local architect Gerald McArdle, and the building has become one of the most striking features of Main Street—a monument to the earliest development of the west end of Fort Wayne on the very eve of its birth in 1840 as an incorporated city.

Structurally, the walls of the 145-year-old house are remarkably sound, and its shape today is much the same as when it was originally built. Over the years, mostly between 1839 and 1874, some changes were made in the main building: the roof was raised about 18 inches and a new, "more modern" Italianate ornamentation added, as was the overhang of the roof. Otherwise the building looks much as it did in 1839.

The man who built this elegant home was William S. Edsall, a fur trader, merchant, contractor, and prominent civic leader. Born in 1811, William was one of the younger sons of Peter Edsall, a poverty-stricken pioneer from New York state. The father died having brought his family as far as Shane's Prairie (present-day Rockford, Ohio), and his wife arrived with their nine children in Fort Wayne in 1824, the year Allen County was organized.

As a young man, William worked with the U.S. corps of topographical engineers which laid out the route of the Wabash and Erie Canal. In 1828 he established a ferry on the St. Mary's River, and then joined the fur trading business of George and W.G. Ewing as a clerk. They sent young Edsall to Huntington as their agent in 1832, and there he was appointed the first postmaster. Two years later William was elected to serve as the first clerk of the counties of Huntington, Wabash, and Whitley.

Edsall returned to Fort Wayne in 1836, and for the next three decades he enjoyed considerable good fortune in business and civic affairs. He joined the Ewings as a partner in the fur trade in 1838, and in 1840 he and his brother Samuel served together as two of Fort Wayne's first city council representatives.

During the 1840s the Edsall brothers operated a major sawmill and a huge flour mill on the canal near the home William had just built on the west end in 1839. The sawmill was located near the West Main Street Bridge; the gristmill by 1850 was the largest of any mill in Fort Wayne. As major contractors and suppliers, the Edsall brothers were involved in most of the major construction projects in town. In 1847 Samuel built the second county courthouse, a two-story brick building with a steeple, as well as the third courthouse in 1861, which served the county until 1895. The most important construction work done by the Edsalls, however, was the Bluffton Plank Road.

Work had already been done by Samuel Edsall to lay a plank road north to Lima, Ohio, but

Far left: Louisa McCarty Edsall lived for 17 years in a house that was very elegant for its time. After she died at the age of 37, her husband William enlarged the house to accommodate the needs of the family, which included four young children. Courtesy, Allen County-Fort Wayne Historical Society

Left: Jenny and Amelia were the daughters of William and Louisa Edsall. Courtesy, Allen County-Fort Wayne Historical Society

the wide expanse of territory south of the county was still all but inaccessible to the business center in Fort Wayne. A convention held in Muncie of farmers and southern merchants decided to make Bellefontaine, Ohio, rather than Fort Wayne, the northeastern end of a rail line out of Indianapolis. The prospect of losing the southern farm trade, especially that of Wells County, spurred Fort Wayne business leaders to agree to subscribe their personal funds to the construction of a surfaced southern road. The contract for this important project was given to the Edsall brothers, who had just completed a steam-powered sawmill, and by 1850 they had built the Bluffton Road for $40,000.

When the railroads came to northern Indiana in the 1850s, the Edsalls again won important construction contracts. The most significant of these was the contract to build the roadbed for the Wabash Railroad on the 43 miles from Ohio to the Wabash River.

Having helped to establish Fort Wayne as a transportation and market center, William Edsall launched his own business as a commission merchant, or broker in produce, fish, and salt. But these were times of financial difficulty. William did not manage his money wisely and incurred heavy debts. He soon lost the Edsall House, put his family up with relatives, and moved to Chicago to be closer to his brokerage affairs.

The house that William made the outward trappings of all that he aspired to was built in 1839. It is a two-story brick building, 44 feet by 20 feet, strictly balanced with two downstairs parlors and two upstairs bedrooms, all separated by a central hall and broad stairway.

Because of further financial troubles, Edsall again lost the house, this time to an area banker who bought it for delinquent taxes at the price of $106. The Edsall family rallied to regain the house and pay off the mortgages, but William did not regain full possession himself until 1874.

At once William had the house "fitted up and furnished throughout in the most elegant style." To celebrate both his homecoming and his sixty-third birthday, Edsall held a huge ball for the "old settlers." The *Sentinel*'s report of the evening affair gives a glimpse of high society life in Fort Wayne 110 years ago:

The many friends of Mr. Edsall during the last few days have been in receipt of invitations for Wednesday evening, April 15th, which indicated an intention to regenerate the old mansion by an elegant and

William S. Edsall was buried in Lindenwood Cemetery, where his stone bears the simple words, "Sad and troubled was his life/May his rest be sweet." Courtesy, Allen County-Fort Wayne Historical Society

fashionable soiree dansante. *About five hundred invitations were sent out, the majority of which met with a ready response, and at 7 o'clock last evening, the full flood of light which streamed from every door and window in the house, and the natural sequence of thronging carriages, the soft rush of encloaked ladies up the stairway, the gleams of dainty slippers and billowy folds of tumultuous white dresses on the way to the dressing room, gave promise of the prolonged pleasure of the night. At half past nine the scene presented was a very brilliant one. The whole house was at the service of the glittering throng of brave men and fair ladies. Music stole through the corridors, and entranced the senses; music, which born of glorious old Johann Strauss, infused the feet to graceful motion and drew the visitors into the voluptuous mazes of the dance, floated in thrilling waves of sound out into the street, and filled the air with melody. The grace of Fort Wayne's women glowed and gleamed within the brilliantly lighted parlors.*

William Edsall lived only two years more, and his funeral took place in the east parlor. When he died in 1876, he once again was broke. The mortgage company assumed ownership of the house,

but for about a year after William's death, his daughter Amelia and her family, as well as his sister Isabella, stayed on, being joined later by three nieces.

In 1878 a movement led by another of Edsall's sisters, Mrs. W.H. Coombs, created City Hospital, which today is known as Parkview Hospital. Organizational and fund-raising meetings for the hospital began in October 1878, and the Edsall House hosted grand opening festivals for the hospital to be built on the grounds nearby. However, the mortgage company would not allow the house to serve as a hospital in the interim. Thus, after a two-day career, the Edsall homestead was abandoned as a hospital site for a mansion on Lewis and Hanna streets. This marked the Edsall family's final association with the property.

William Edsall's obituary proclaimed that no man had been more intimately connected with the growth of the city and with its improvements than he, and that a sketch of his life is really a sketch of Fort Wayne from the time it was a mere Indian trading post. The same could be said about the home that he built, for it today is the only concrete link with the years of the city's beginnings.

THE WILDWOOD NEIGHBORHOODS

Two of the best-known neighborhoods in Fort Wayne, Wildwood Park and Lafayette Place, were among the city's earliest subdivisions. Both, too, were the pride and joy of Fort Wayne's first advocates of city planning, Lee J. Ninde and his wife, Joel Roberts Ninde.

Wildwood Park today is the plush hilltop development that centers on North Washington Road between Jefferson Boulevard and the Fort Wayne Country Club. Comfortable homes on spacious grounds fill this neighborhood that is distinctive not only for its winding roads but also for its site on the only real hill in Fort Wayne. This hill is part of the range of hillocks that rise in the Maumee Valley and march southwest into the Wabash

Far left: Arthur A. Shurtleff came to Fort Wayne to be part of the Wildwood development. Born in Boston, Massachusetts, he attended Boston High School, M.I.T., and Harvard University, where he studied his profession under the best teachers in the country. Before coming to Fort Wayne, he traveled extensively in England, Germany, Holland, France, Belgium, Italy, and the Azores to study private parks, estates, playgrounds, and waterfronts. Shurtleff is responsible for the transformation of a number of barren places into blooming gardens and pleasant vistas. From Wildwood Magazine, 1914. Courtesy, Allen County-Fort Wayne Historical Society

Left: The energy and encouragement that Lee J. Ninde gave to the new art of city planning has helped it take root in hundreds of American cities. Ninde was born in Fort Wayne on Janurary 8, 1874. After leaving high school he attended Phillips Exeter Academy and Harvard University, where he received his law degree in 1895. When he returned to Fort Wayne, Ninde practiced law for 10 years before organizing the Wildwood Builders Company in 1910. From Griswold, The Builders of Greater Fort Wayne, 1926. Courtesy, Allen County-Fort Wayne Historical Society

Valley. It is, in fact, a watershed—a continental divide—marking the separation of the drainage system, on the east, to the Lake Erie basin and, on the west, to the Ohio and Mississippi River basin.

To the pioneer settlers in the early nineteenth century, these small hills west of Fort Wayne were too steep and too heavily wooded in oak, hickory, and elm trees to be worth the effort to tame them. In the years around the turn of the century, however, the area became popular as a picnic spot for Fort Wayne adventurers who dared to make the trek from the city by horse and buggy along the old canal route to the wilderness farm. Picnickers then also had to pass the infamous Bootjack, a house of ill repute, which actually added spice to the day's outing.

Just before the outbreak of World War I, in 1910, the local realtor Lee J. Ninde, inspired by the architectural work of his wife, Joel Roberts Ninde, formed the Wildwood Builders Company and purchased the Hoffman farm for $38,000. The company hired the Boston planner Arthur A. Shurtleff to develop the layout for the new residential community the Nindes had in mind. This was the first time a nationally recognized architect had been brought

to Fort Wayne to lay out an addition to the city. Prior to this, all additions, indeed all city planning, was done in the neoclassical grid pattern adapted from the ancient Romans. Little or no attention was given to the needs for landscaping, parks, or playgrounds, or to the quality of housing—planners were concerned only with the lots themselves. Aesthetically, the old grid pattern was based on the symmetry of ordered blocks ranging from the central square; alleyways were the usual provision for "out-of-sight" functions. Sanitation was often an afterthought, and standing trees were uprooted so that saplings could be replanted in an orderly fashion.

The Wildwood Company excited Fort Wayne

by creating a new kind of residential development. Wildwood Park, for instance, would have no straight, grid-patterned streets, nor any alleyways. Trees would be spared wherever possible, and carefully nursed back to health when necessary. The roads would follow natural contours rather than be graded to "improve Nature"; these winding roads would discourage speeding and, above all, add to the aesthetic appearance of the neighborhood. All this marked wholesale revolt against the established pattern.

Furthermore, although long exposure to prairie land had convinced most Hoosiers that any lot not exactly on street level was a failure, none of the Wildwood lots conformed to that expectation, and either terraced or sunken gardens were planned everywhere. In addition, a neighborhood water supply was developed, the pump house for many years acting as "the secret club house" for children who lived there. A well-planned double sewage system was also developed, one for surface drainage and another, deeper one for household waste. Another novelty of the Wildwood Company development was its official exclusivity. By company rules no house under a certain value could be built in the development (then, the smallest value allowed was $6,500); and no saloons, mercantile houses, hogpens, asylums, cattle yards, chicken coops, or graveyards could be built there.

These novel ideas did not gain popularity quickly in Fort Wayne, and growth in Wildwood was slow—so slow that some called it Hungry Hill. As late as 1923 there still were only seven houses in the tract. Partly this was due to the place being "so far out in the country." The extension of the streetcar lines and then the paved highway of Jefferson Boulevard West changed all that in the late 1920s, however, and Wildwood Park grew rapidly into the more densely populated neighborhood that it has become since World War II.

East of the St. Mary's River the other strikingly new development in suburban planning by the Nindes was Lafayette Place, on the southern outskirts of Fort Wayne along the old Piqua Plank Road. In 1915 its 75 acres of wooded grounds and natural pasturage was again laid out by the Boston landscape architect Arthur Shurtleff. The distinctive feature in this flat land development was the Esplanade, a half-mile strip of park through the middle of the tract. Setting aside such a park area for the sole sake of beauty and recreation was a completely new concept in residential planning, and best illustrates the Nindes' ideas about the need to blend aesthetics and function in everyday life. At the Esplanade's northern end a neighborhood center was planned although never actually built, with parlors, pool tables, and tennis courts to encourage "neighborliness."

Such was the enthusiasm for the concept of neighborliness that the original investors formed the city's first neighborhood association. Just as today, annual dues by property owners were collected to ensure that sidewalks would be shoveled in winter and the common grounds maintained in summer. Just as in Wildwood, investment minimums were aimed at ensuring the quality of neighborhood life. Meanwhile, the class of people targeted to settle in Lafayette Place would be reassured to find that lots had almost no room for a backyard, a sure sign of affluence in that families did not need to grow their own vegetables.

The guiding hands behind the concept of planned neighborhoods that put quality of community life in the forefront were Lee and Joel Ninde. Lee J. Ninde had given up the legal profession to pursue his fascination with urban planning. He was born in 1874, the son of Judge Lindley and Beulah Ninde, whose home on Fairfield Avenue became the nucleus for the Lutheran Hospital. In 1895 Lee graduated from Harvard with a degree in law and returned to Fort Wayne to practice with his father and his brother Dan. He married Joel Roberts in 1900, and within 10 years he had relinquished the bar and thrown himself into the neighborhood development movement. To promote this movement he and his wife formed the Wildwood Builders Company in 1910, and in 1914 began the publication of the prestigious magazine, *The Wildwood,* as a forum for city planning ideas across the nation.

The Nindes' great enterprise eventually convinced state lawmakers to enact legislation that would encourage localities to create city planning commissions. The struggle had lasted from 1917 to 1921, primarily as a campaign to educate legislators about the modern science of planned city building. Immediately upon passage of the legislation in 1921, the leading towns across Indiana—South Bend, Indianapolis, Terre Haute, Lafayette, Kokomo, and Evansville—all created city planning commissions. But to Lee Ninde's great humiliation, his own hometown of Fort Wayne refused for three years to accept the idea. At last, in 1924, Fort Wayne became the last Indiana city to begin formal urban planning.

Lee Ninde's inspiration was Joel Roberts Ninde, his wife. Joel Roberts was born in Mobile, Alabama, in 1874, and she came at a young age to Indianapolis where she married Lee Ninde. Raised in traditional fashion, Joel Ninde had no formal training in architecture, but she was so repulsed by the "mail-order houses" of most neighborhoods, or the "silly ostentation of useless gingerbread" homes with their plate glass doors and garish Victorian colors, that she began utilizing her considerable painting talents in the design of aesthetic but utilitarian homes. No sooner would she design and build one of her "artistic cottages" with its characteristic profile of a handsome barn, than she would be swamped with hopeful buyers. "Mrs. Ninde's houses" became the talk of the city, and this led to the Wildwood development and her husband's involvement in the business.

Lee Ninde became the promoter and realtor while Joel Ninde and her partner, Grace E. Crosby, created the designs and supervised the construc-

Joel Roberts Ninde did not set out to become an architect. However, as she designed and built the house of her dreams, she found that others wished to purchase it. The first houses she designed were simple, charming cottages. As the whole city talked about "Mrs. Ninde's houses," the demand for her services grew. In time, she moved from designing houses to designing entire neighborhoods. From Wildwood Magazine, *1916. Courtesy, Allen County-Fort Wayne Historical Society*

tion. Typical of their approach was their "house of convenience," a model upon which much of their work was based. This model home was designed to show off the Nindes' characteristic blend of economical building materials, durability, and good looks. This was a home in which the housekeeper was the main focus and in which individualism was deemed available to the modest home as well as to the opulent. Thus began the realization of the middle-class dream of home ownership as a source of pride, self-identity, and creativity.

Joel Ninde died young, at age 42, on March 7, 1916. But not before she had left a deep impression on a young generation of designers—and homebuyers—who were to throw over the old regime in domestic architecture. A new generation

This portrait of Thomas and Lucy Swinney was taken by photograher B.H. Benham. Courtesy, Allen County-Fort Wayne Historical Society

of architects was inspired by the fact that she had received no formal training, that it was the good taste of the contemporary artist rather than the canon of the past master that had guided her influential work.

THE TRIER ENTERPRISE

Swinney Park is one of the oldest and best-known recreation sites in Fort Wayne. The original park, on the eastern side of the St. Mary's River, is centered on the old Swinney Homestead. For many years this was the museum of the Allen County-Fort Wayne Historical Society, and today it is home to those who are devoted to restoring the old mansion. Across the river is the 48-acre tract known as West Swinney Park, and here activities revolve around the public swimming pool and the large playing fields.

Thomas Swinney, who made the original be-

quest of land to the city, came to Fort Wayne before 1824 from Piketon, Ohio, where he had been born in 1803. As a farmer determined to develop a large estate, Swinney bought land along the east bank of the St. Mary's soon after his arrival. But the first of two principal parcels of land came to him through his marriage, in 1827, to Lucy Taber. She had received the land which was to be the future site of the homestead and East Swinney Park from her father, Paul Taber, the man who laid out the second extension of Fort Wayne, known as Taber's Addition. Swinney then acquired the second major portion of land from Lucy's brother, Cyrus Taber, after Cyrus moved to Logansport. This was the large tract that nearly 80 years later would become West Swinney Park.

In the years that followed, during the 1830s and 1840s, Thomas and Lucy Swinney became prominent figures in the growing community. Thomas served twice as Allen County treasurer, as justice of the peace, and as "overseer of the poor." The couple's beautiful Federal style home and wooded grounds became known as one of the most attractive sites in Fort Wayne.

Such already was its park-like allure that on July 4, 1843, on the occasion of the long-awaited opening of the Wabash and Erie Canal, the Swinney farm was used for the great dedication festivities. At the end of the ceremonies, the crowd was treated to a barbecue provided by Peter Kaiser, a civic enthusiast who had gone all the way to Lafayette to purchase two oxen for the feast. Kaiser had planned, appropriately enough, to bring the oxen back by the newly opened canal, but the beasts refused to go aboard the boat and Kaiser had to drive the animals on foot the entire 110 miles back to Fort Wayne—a trip that lasted 11 days. Peter Kaiser no doubt looked forward to the barbecue with a certain vindictive pleasure.

In later years Thomas Swinney presented the east homestead property to Fort Wayne. By the terms of his bequest the city would receive the land after the death of his daughters, Caroline and Frances, who still lived in the old home. In preparation for this anxiously awaited event, the city park board bought several lots south of the Swinney homestead in 1869. But even before Thomas Swinney died, on January 20, 1875, the land got a taste of its future use. In 1874 the Allen County Fair was established on a portion of the spacious grounds when the newly formed Allen County Fair Association rented the land. A half-mile race track was laid out and the whole area enclosed, with entry gates at both Washington and Jefferson streets. The first horse races were held in June 1874, and the annual fair opened that September, as it would do for many years thereafter, to crowds in the thousands. More than a decade later, reflecting the booming industrial growth of Fort Wayne, the first Labor Day celebration was held in Fort Wayne at the Swinney property in 1889, although Indiana as a state did not recognize the holiday until 1891. A large parade ended at the fairgrounds where Mrs. E.C. Williams, an organizer of one of the early labor unions, the Knights of Labor, was the main speaker.

The spectacular growth in land and popularity of the Swinney Park area came, however, after 1918 when the park department, under superintendent Adolph Jaenicke, bought the 48 acres west of the St. Mary's River for $37,000. Shortly after West Swinney was purchased, a part of the park was leased to George Trier, who developed the amusement concessions. So popular did this part of West Swinney become, as the city's only amusement park, that from the 1920s on, the place was commonly known as Trier's Park.

George F. Trier was born in Fort Wayne in 1876, a year after Thomas Swinney died. His grandparents and his parents had been Allen County settlers from as early as the 1820s. Trier was educated in one of the Fort Wayne Lutheran schools and at the newly founded, in 1889, International Business College, a precursor of Indiana

George F. Trier was born in Fort Wayne on November 8, 1876, to Henry and Wilhelmina Trier. George began his business career as a stenographer, but after his marriage to Estella Mulqueen he turned to managing her dancing school. After conducting a successful dance pavilion at Robison Park, north of the city, he expanded his operations by leasing an entire city park—an undertaking which attracted national attention. In West Swinney Park George Trier managed his dance school, conducted a public dance pavilion, and provided a great variety of outdoor amusements and facilities for picnics, reunions, and celebrations. From Griswold, The Builders of Greater Fort Wayne, *1926. Courtesy, Allen County-Fort Wayne Historical Society*

Above: The American Coaster Slide in Swinney Park is pictured in action. In 1916 there were five such slides in the park system; it took one carpenter two weeks each summer just to repair and maintain the wooden structures. Courtesy, Allen County-Fort Wayne Historical Society

Right: The latest in 1930s swimwear is on display in this photograph taken at the West Swinney Park Pool. Courtesy, Allen County-Fort Wayne Historical Society

Tech. After graduation he held a variety of office jobs, from stenographer to bookkeeper. In 1895 he joined the National Telegraph Company as a secretary, but by 1897 he had become general manager of the company. In 1902, when the Home Telephone Company took over, Trier took the position of general manager of the Delaware and Madison Counties Telephone Company. During these years in the business world, Trier met Estella Mulqueen, who had just established a dancing school in Fort Wayne. George Trier was one of her first pupils. His fascination with ballroom dancing and Miss Mulqueen led Trier to abandon his telephone career in order to devote all his attentions to the dance (and, of course, to Estella).

Trier became quite proficient at formal dancing, and he soon married Estella. Together the couple established one of the most successful dance studios in the Midwest. In 1911 the Triers built their own facility, the Minuet Building, at 121 East Washington, and by 1916 the Trier Academy of Dancing had grown to an annual enrollment of nearly 800 pupils. In 1905, because of his "conviction to elevate the standard of the American ballroom and to provide for the people clean, healthful amusement," Trier opened a dance pavilion at Robison Park, then the favorite entertainment spot in town. So popular was this ballroom, especially for summer dances, that he enlarged the building in 1914. In 1920 Robison Park was closed, and the Triers moved their dance pavilion to West Swinney Park. But this time he also bought many of the old amusement rides there, most notably The Cyclone, a roller coaster. The cost to Trier was more than $125,000.

In the following decades, Swinney Park was a major Fort Wayne attraction, especially on Kid's Day, when prices were slashed. By 1949, Fort Wayne families could enjoy pony rides, bumper cars, a merry-go-round, Harry Glidden's miniature train, The Cyclone, a penny arcade, root beer, popcorn, and hot dogs. True to the Fort Wayne Park Department's fortunate penchant for building beautiful flower gardens, the Japanese Gardens (later, the Jaenicke Gardens, named after landscaper Adolph Jaenicke) were, like today's Lakeside, a favorite spot for strollers, lovers, and blossom thieves.

The spectacular end of Swinney Park came over 35 years ago. In June 1953 the dance hall, roller coaster, and fun house were destroyed by fire. Today the park is a much quieter place. The screams of Cyclone riders have been replaced by the playful shouts of children around the pool or on the ball fields, and there are no more horse races. But neither are there summer dances hosted by George Trier and Estella Mulqueen.

The picturesque entrance to Swinney Park is shown in 1911. Courtesy, Allen County-Fort Wayne Historical Society

*This turn-of-the-century Fort Wayne office was spacious,
pleasantly appointed, and cool. Courtesy, Allen County-Fort
Wayne Historical Society*

CHAPTER SIX

Partners in Progress

Studying business and industry within a community reveals much about the character of that city.

Fort Wayne has been abundantly blessed with many firms whose products and services reflect a strong response to local, regional, and national growth and goals. It is no coincidence that their leaders have been men and women of considerable character and compassion.

Located at the confluence of the Maumee, St. Joseph, and St. Marys rivers, Fort Wayne became home to businesses and industries whose growth was closely linked to the availability of water. Pioneer industries relying heavily on the accessibility of the rivers were succeeded by increasingly sophisticated enterprises, which today rely on the most modern of twentieth-century technology to thrive and prosper. In this city of the three rivers, economic life and leadership have also flourished.

Nourishment for such growth came from precedents established by business and community leaders of earlier eras. Their successors act upon an awareness that a city's future hinges on its ability to employ the strength of its convictions.

Almost invariably, companies whose histories reflect durable growth and development in Fort Wayne are those who have looked beyond their own immediate interests to consider, and embrace, community endeavors. Business histories reveal that corporate leaders have pursued a tradition of contributing time, money, and talent to social and cultural endeavors. They have helped build not only Fort Wayne's economy but, just as essential, her soul.

While circumstances occasionally have necessitated the departure or demise of some industrial and commercial entities in Fort Wayne, there has been no long-term diminishment of spirit, nor room in the city's mentality to entertain economic depression. New ventures have been courted, and large and small businesses lured to or founded in the city; the community's high standard of living and expectations of continuing future growth remain alive and well. Soon aware of the importance in Fort Wayne of community involvement, newcomers in business and industry quickly adopt the attitude that living and working in the city involve contributing to its overall welfare. Within the decade of the 1980s this dominant attitude has been a significant factor in the city earning two national accolades: All-America City and Most Livable City.

Today Fort Wayne is not only at the hub of three rivers, but also is the focal point of a major metropolitan area. Yet it is still possible to find obvious traces of yesteryear's charm in many neighborhoods where old homes overlook brick-lined streets leading to nearby businesses and industries. Citizen and corporation live together compatibly. Fort Wayne has been, is, and hopefully always will be a city where business and resident are the very best of neighbors.

The organizations whose stories are detailed on the following pages have chosen to support this important literary and civic project. They illustrate the variety of ways in which individuals and their businesses have contributed to the area's growth and development. The civic involvement of Fort Wayne's businesses, institutions of health and of learning, and local government, in cooperation with its citizens, has made Allen County an excellent place to live and work.

99

ALLEN COUNTY-FORT WAYNE HISTORICAL SOCIETY

Historic Fort Wayne portrays in "Living History" life at the fort in 1816, the year Indiana became a state.

As the Allen County-Fort Wayne Historical Society observes its 67th year of service to the community in 1988, it continues to enjoy celebrating its own, as well as others', historic endeavors.

Michael C. Hawfield, executive director, describes the history museum as the "community's mirror and its official portrait" through which it is charged by charter to promote and augment the "teaching of history as well as the education of the public in history."

Founded in 1921 by a group of Fort Wayne citizens, the organization was housed until 1980 in the stately Thomas W. Swinney homestead, located on a site overlooking Swinney Park and the nearby St. Mary's River. Among early accomplishments of the society were the development and placement of historical site markers throughout Allen County, publication of materials on many diverse history-related topics, and preservation of significant historical materials and memorabilia. Twice in the society's 67 years it has received national recognition by the American Association for State and Local History for excellence in historical preservation efforts.

The society directed research and financing for the establishment of Historic Fort Wayne, a replica of the fort built and occupied in 1816 under the direction of Major John Whistler. The fort today is considered one of the North American continent's "best interpreted historic sites," and annually is visited by people from throughout the world. In early 1986 Historic Fort Wayne and the historical society united so that each organization could, through close cooperative efforts, improve programming and financial bases. Efforts are under way to acquire national accreditation of the museum and fort.

A major step forward in the society's own history occurred when the organization acquired and, in 1980 relocated to, the former city hall building at East Berry and Barr streets, within one block of other major arts facilities in downtown Fort Wayne. Renovation of the structure, built in 1893, was undertaken at a cost of more than one million dollars; today it houses the museum's research library, archive of historical documents and photographs, and collection of relics, including an outstanding collection of Indiana "primitive" paintings.

Today the society's net worth exceeds more than $4.5 million; increased financial support for maintenance and repair of the museum building and fort has been committed by community arts campaigns. Business support also is being strengthened, as the society remains focused on its goal of making history come alive for present and future generations. Helping in this regard are performing artists in theater and music who take an active role in innovative programming endeavors, and the Barr Street Irregulars, whose volunteer efforts raise funds for various museum projects. In 1986-1987 volunteers, crucial to the ongoing strength of the museum and fort, contributed more than 15,000 hours of service for an in-kind contribution of more than $64,000.

The Allen County-Fort Wayne Historical Society is located in the former city hall building, which also houses The Calaboose Gallery, Fort Wayne's old jail.

FORT WAYNE NATIONAL BANK

Businesses have come and gone in downtown Fort Wayne, but one that has remained an enduring landmark for all of its 55 years of service is Fort Wayne National Bank.

Opening for business on October 30, 1933, at 123 West Berry Street, the bank remained at that site until 1970, when it relocated across the street to a newly constructed, 26-story building at 110 West Berry Street. Occupying a portion of what is now the city's second-tallest structure, Fort Wayne National Bank remains a focal point of the business communities of Fort Wayne and northeastern Indiana.

Founded by James M. Barrett, Jr., H.J. Bowerfind, Walter S. Goll, Gaylord Leslie, L.H. Moore, Fred B. Shoaff, and Edward M. Wilson, the

The founders chose Fred S. Hunting to head the bank. He held that position for eight years, and then went on to serve as chairman of the board until 1948.

bank initially was under the executive leadership of Fred S. Hunting, a retired head of the Fort Wayne operation of General Electric Company. With Depression-era bank failures still clear in the memories of potential depositors, the founders of the Fort Wayne National Bank wisely chose Hunting, a nonbanker, to allay those fears. He led the institution as president for its initial eight years of operation and served as chairman of the board until 1948. He was succeeded as president by Wendell C. Laycock.

Under the leadership of Hunting, Laycock, Russell Daane, and, since 1969, Paul E. Shaffer, chairman of the board and chief executive officer, Fort Wayne National became a full-service bank that today operates 17 offices throughout Allen County. Its international banking department serves many local and area firms engaged in foreign enterprise.

In 1933 Fort Wayne National Bank's resources were $5.58 million. Within 10 years that amount rose to $43.7 million. By December 1986 resources totaled more than $1.19 billion.

Serving as an integral part of area business endeavors, Fort Wayne National takes pride in its continuing involvement in the development of downtown Fort Wayne. Its officers, directors, and employees, true to the tradition established by the founders, continue to assume active leadership roles in the community.

The institution serves as host for a community event that draws several hundred thousand spectators. Each July a dazzling fireworks display is launched from the roof of the bank building as the concluding event of the nine-day Three Rivers Festival.

Current officers and directors of Fort Wayne National Bank are Paul E. Shaffer, chairman of the board and chief executive officer; Jackson R.

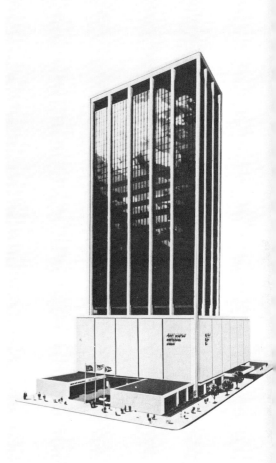

Fort Wayne National Bank, located at 110 West Berry Street, occupies a portion of what is now the city's second-tallest structure. The bank was established in 1933, and continues to serve the area of Fort Wayne and northeastern Indiana.

Lehman, president and chief administrative officer; Walter S. Ainsworth; James M. Barrett III; Richard B. Doner; David C. Genever-Watling; Thomas C. Griffith; Donald B. Grissom; Michael C. Haggerty; Bob F. Jesse; Lynn A. Koehlinger; G. Irving Latz II; Kenneth W. Maxfield; Carl W. Moellering; Amy B. Morrill; James A. O'Connor; Max P. Shambaugh; Thomas M. Shoaff; and Don A. Wolf.

CARPETLAND USA

The carpeting store that opened its doors in Fort Wayne in October 1932 is, some 56 years later, believed to be the city's oldest carpeting establishment.

Known originally as Standard Rug and Linoleum when founded by Fred Lipp, the firm's name was changed in 1969 to Carpetland USA. Fred Lipp, joined in the business by his son Stan in 1960, witnessed many changes within the business before his death in 1982.

In years past, his son explains, wool was the dominant fiber; today it is nylon. Linoleum disappeared in the 1960s, replaced by stronger, more versatile vinyl products. The Lipps also found carpet being used much more extensively—indoors and outdoors, on walls, and in businesses that 40 or more years ago would have utilized wood, linoleum, or tile flooring.

"In the old days," Stan Lipp says, "sources for wool were many; there were many manufacturing companies producing carpet, all of them reasonably small. Today the greatest amount of business is being done by larger companies, while there are many peripheral firms. Our products are basically 'made-in-America' products. In the beginning the home was the focal point. Today hospitals, stores, offices, and theaters utilize carpet and other coverings."

Fred Lipp opened his store in Fort Wayne after learning more about the carpet and linoleum business from a brother and his partner in their Indianapolis firm. Standard Rug moved several times in downtown Fort Wayne; one move, in 1948, was necessitated by a fire that totally destroyed the store. The Lipps opened a second store, at Northcrest Shopping Center, in the 1960s to serve people who no longer patronized downtown stores. However, the store closed within five years; ample parking space at the family's new

downtown location at 330 West Jefferson attracted customers downtown once again. The store moved to its present site at 1111 West Washington Center Road in 1973.

When Stan Lipp joined his father in the business, the organization encompassed 15 stores, situated in Colorado, Minnesota, Illinois, Kentucky, Ohio, Missouri, and Indiana. Under the younger Lipp's guidance, the corporate name was changed to Carpetland USA, and operations refocused on some 55 companyowned and franchised businesses. Currently Stan Lipp is part owner of the franchise system and owner of the Fort Wayne business.

The Fort Wayne store, which encompasses some 21,000 square feet,

Known originally as Standard Rug and Linoleum, Carpetland USA was founded by Fred Lipp in Fort Wayne in 1932.

serves customers in Ohio, Michigan, Indiana, and even abroad. A Russian ballet troupe entertaining in Fort Wayne purchased carpet at the store to take home with them. Another highlight in the store's history was carpeting the bus of longtime entertainer Fred Waring.

Stan Lipp, recently appointed to the board of Fort Wayne Community Schools, says the "most satisfying" part of the business for him has been to "help make customers' homes more beautiful. The business also has given me the freedom to pursue civic activities."

ITT AEROSPACE/OPTICAL DIVISION

ITT Aerospace/Optical Division is among the electronics-related firms drawn to Fort Wayne some 40 years ago. The division is one of seven in the ITT Defense Technology Corporation, a leading supplier of high-technology command, control, and communications; electronic defense; electro-optical; and surveillance systems and related services for the United States and friendly foreign governments.

ITT is a diversified, multinational company that manufactures and sells automotive, electronic component, fluid technology, defense, space, and natural resources products, as well as provides and sells insurance, hotel, financial, communication information, and community development services. ITT also has a 37-percent interest in the world's largest telecommunications manufacturing company, Alcatel N.V.

The Aerospace/Optical Division in Fort Wayne grew out of ITT's acquisition of the Capehart and Farnsworth radio and television facilities in 1949. No ITT history would be complete without recognition of Philo Farnsworth, who, in 1927 at age 20, transmitted and received the first all-electronic television image.

In 1938 Farnsworth moved from San Francisco to Philadelphia and then to Fort Wayne; purchased the Capehart Company, which manufactured phonographs; and continued his work under the corporate name of Farnsworth Television and Radio Corporation. That same year he was granted a patent on his invention, and after a public demonstration, he was considered to be the Father of Television.

Credited with the development and manufacture of many industrial and commercial products, Farnsworth made significant contributions to the World War II effort. His work, which was undertaken in collaboration with his colleagues,

While still attending high school Philo Farnsworth became enchanted with the idea of transmitting moving pictures by electricity. A few years later he developed the image dissector camera using electronics, signaling the beginning of television as we know it today.

played a key role in missile-guidance and early-warning systems. In 1948 Farnsworth returned to Fort Wayne where Farnsworth Television and Radio was attempting to meet the demand for television sets. However, the company had to rely on parts manufactured and controlled by an adversary, RCA, and delays were causing financial problems for Farnsworth. To avoid bankruptcy, the firm was sold to ITT, which subsequently

phased out television except for industrial purposes. Prior to his death in 1971, Farnsworth devoted his attention to nuclear fusion, for which he was granted two patents; altogether, he held some 165 patents.

At the time of acquisition ITT created the Capehart-Farnsworth Corporation. In 1956 the Capehart portion was sold, with ITT retaining Farnsworth Electronics Company. Subsequent reorganizations led to what has been known since 1969 as the Aerospace/Optical Division.

ITT Aerospace/Optical Division still uses the original Farnsworth facilities at 3700 East Pontiac Street and has expanded into additional facilities in Fort Wayne. The division encompasses engineering, research and development, and complete production facilities. It is the nation's largest supplier of air traffic control communications equipment, a primary supplier of meteorological instruments for environmental satellites, and the developer and producer of the U.S. Army's new Combat Net Radio called SINCGARS (Single Channel Ground and Airborne Radio System).

ITT Aerospace/Optical Division still uses the original Farnsworth facilities at 3700 East Pontiac Street.

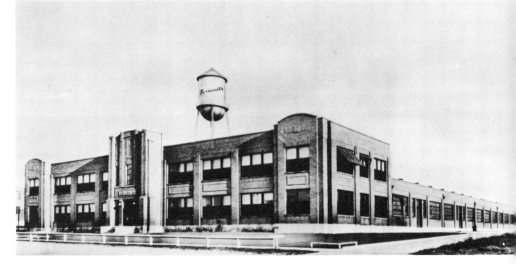

DANA CORPORATION SPICER AXLE DIVISION

Fort Wayne became home in 1946 to the first plant constructed by the Dana Corporation specifically for the production of car and truck axles. The parent company had grown through the leadership of Charles A. Dana, a prosecuting attorney from New York City who had successfully reorganized the Spicer Manufacturing Corporation, founded in 1903 by Clarence Winfred Spicer in Plainfield, New Jersey.

As a mechanical engineering student at Cornell University, Spicer had devised a drive shaft, employing tubing and universal joints, that became popular with the new automobile industry. His sales grew, and within 10 years he moved operations to a new plant in South Plainfield. However, as competition grew, Spicer experienced financial difficulties. Within two years after Dana reorganized the firm, it was again on solid ground, thanks also to the end of World War I and the burgeoning of the trucking industry.

Dana added products and companies, the latter including the Salisbury Axle Company of Jamestown, New York. In 1929 the corporation relocated to Toledo, Ohio, for closer access to the automotive and trucking industry in Detroit. The company continued to grow, and corporate leaders saw the need for a new plant specifically for manufacturing axles. Fort Wayne was selected as the new site; following completion of construction, all axle work was transferred from Toledo to Fort Wayne.

On April 12, 1946, the first shipment of axles was made to the Studebaker Corporation in South Bend, Indiana. Fred Shepler, who was to work for the company for 40 years, was among the first 250 employees hired. He was just out of World War II military service and eager for work. Dana, he explains, "was a new plant and offered a good opportunity to advance. All the other plants in Fort Wayne were old; if you got in at Dana on the ground floor, you could move up real easy." He remembers his take-home pay in the early days was $38.

Marie Moser, a 41-year employee, was one of no more than six women working in the office years ago. Attracted to the company because of favorable pay and benefits, she fared well. Originally hired as a keypunch operator, she moved into management and currently administers management payroll.

The two longtime employees say there has always been a family atmosphere at Dana; retirees tend to return frequently to see former co-workers and to participate in various activities.

The plant, at 2424 West State Boulevard, expanded from its original 225,000 square feet to encompass 1,156,707 square feet, or about 31.34 acres. The Spicer Axle Division today employs 2,154 men and women, including 1,707 hourly employees who belong to the Allied Industrial Workers Union. The average length of service is 15 years.

As part of one of the 105 largest industrial corporations in the United States and one of the 250 largest in the world, the division manufactured and shipped 1,116,577 axles in 1986. Its top five customers are Ford, AMC, GMC, Chrysler, and International Service. Annual export sales total $22 million.

The Dana Corporation Spicer Axle Division plant, at 2424 West State Boulevard, expanded from its original 225,000 square feet to its current 1,156,707 square feet (about 31.34 acres).

CENTRAL SOYA COMPANY, INC.

Central Soya Company, Inc., a mainstay of the Fort Wayne business community for more than 50 years, was "born" in October 1934 in Decatur, Indiana, a community 25 miles south of Fort Wayne.

Dale W. McMillen, Sr., a pioneer in the concentrated feed business and president of Allied Mills in Fort Wayne, was looking for a new challenge at age 54. He found it in the abandoned Central Sugar Mill in Decatur. McMillen, widely known as "Mr. Mac," restored beet-sugar-processing operations and added soybean processing, a combination that produced soybean meal, beet pulp, and molasses, three important ingredients for livestock feed.

The company became a leader in the marketing of feed concentrates as an alternative to traditional livestock feeds and was among the first to process soybeans by the solvent-extraction method. Within 20 years net sales reached $150 million, 2,000 people were employed, and annual soybean-processing capacity had grown to 20 million bushels. Feed-manufacturing capabilities surpassed one million tons.

In the 1950s Central Soya established a grain-merchandising operation to buy and sell grain and soybeans, and to purchase soybeans for processing. The firm was the first to ship bulk feed by rail in its own covered hopper cars; it used its own fleet of barges to transport grain by water. Acquiring the Chemurgy Divi-

Central Soya's original Decatur, Indiana, plant, shown in its early years of operation, had its beginnings in an abandoned Central Sugar mill.

sion of the Glidden Company, Central Soya added two large soybean-processing plants, 11 million bushels of storage capacity, and 523 employees. It also expanded its product line to soy protein and lecithin, and acquired extensive research facilities. The company was the first to commercialize soy-protein isolate and soy-protein concentrates as food ingredients.

The firm continued to prosper under the leadership of Mr. Mac's sons, Harold W. and Dale W. Jr. Plants opened in Illinois, Tennessee, Ohio, and Pennsylvania; facilities expanded at McMillen Feed in Decatur. The firm's first plant outside the continental United States opened in Puerto Rico in 1964. Later plants

The Decatur, Indiana, operation as it is today. The company has 65 plants and facilities worldwide, and employs approximately 3,500 people.

were opened in Trinidad and other international locations, including several in Europe. The firm was serving feed customers in 51 countries by the early 1970s.

The 1970s saw Central Soya enter the institutional foods business and open edible vegetable oil refineries in Decatur and Chattanooga, Tennessee. Retail food processing came with the acquisition of J.H. Filbert, Inc., in 1972, and a new research and engineering center opened six years later at Indiana 3 and Cook Road in Fort Wayne. Additional plants served new markets in the Midwest and West.

In 1985 the firm was bought by Shamrock Capital, L.P., part of the Roy Disney holdings, and corporate reorganization included divestiture of some earlier acquisitions and renewed focus on the core businesses of soybean processing and animal feeds. Two years later Central Soya was sold to the agribusiness giant Ferruzzi Group of Ravenna, Italy, a sale valued at $170 million. At the time of sale Central Soya Company, Inc., employed 3,500 people throughout the world; fiscal 1986 reports showed sales of $1.38 billion.

LINCOLN FOODSERVICE PRODUCTS, INC.

In 1987 Lincoln Foodservice Products, Inc., celebrated its 30th year of business in Fort Wayne where, in June 1957, it began operations under the name of Lincoln Manufacturing Company, Inc. Lincoln initially functioned as designer, consultant, and middleman between the fabricator and end users of food-service equipment.

Flourishing under the leadership of founder and company president D. Dean Rhoads, the firm moved, in 1964, from its original site at 3232 Calhoun Street to a newly constructed 45,000-square-foot manufacturing plant at 1425 Progress Road. The company continued to prosper, due in large part to its development of modular food-service equipment designed to reduce labor costs in school lunch programs.

By 1971 the firm employed 70 people and an additional 10 food-service manufacturing representatives. That same year the Aluminum Company of America (Alcoa) purchased 50-percent ownership of Lincoln and began construction of a 228,000-square-foot building at 1111 North Hadley Road. By 1976 the entire business was relocated to that site. Before retiring in 1977, Rhoads sold his interest to Alcoa, making Lincoln a wholly owned subsidiary of Alcoa.

In 1982 Lincoln management and certain investors associated

Lincoln Foodservice Products, Inc., is located at 1111 North Hadley Road. Its well-known brand-name products include Wear-Ever, Centurion, Impinger, Fresh-o-matic, and Galley.

with Wesray Corporation of Morristown, New Jersey, purchased the firm from Alcoa. The company changed its name to Lincoln Foodservice Products, Inc., and became a publicly held corporation in 1986.

Growth in the conveyorized oven business necessitated the addition of more than 130,000 square feet of warehouse, manufacturing, and office space in the mid-1980s. Between 1981 and 1985 gross sales rose from $19.5 million to $45.4 million.

Today, under the direction of board chairman and president Gordon D. Bell, the company is one of the nation's largest manufacturers of conveyor ovens and aluminum food-service utensils, marketed through a 25-member sales staff and approximately 1,500 distributors in the United States and abroad. Its products are marketed under the brand names of Wear-Ever, Centurion, Impinger, Fresh-o-matic, and Galley. The Fort Wayne-based firm currently employs 360 people.

Officers in addition to Bell are William A. Thomas, executive vice-president/operations; Roy M. Rentz, vice-president and chief financial officer; James N. Shaffer, vice-president/materials management; John C. Heithaus, vice-president/marketing and new business development; John V. Butler, vice-president/sales; Robert F. Plattner, vice-president/research and engineering; and David O. Cole, vice-president and controller.

Lincoln Foodservice Products is known as one of the leading manufacturers of conveyor ovens and food-service utensils. Shown here is the Impinger Oven.

BROTHERHOOD MUTUAL INSURANCE COMPANY

The corporate goal of Brotherhood Mutual Insurance Company remains the same as it was in 1917: serving policyholders with an attitude of compassion, courtesy, and concern.

Paul A. Steiner, president, says the service-oriented company grew out of a church constituency—Evangelical Mennonite—and that heritage continues to be a guiding force. Today the firm insures nearly 12,000 churches in a 19-state service area, including New Mexico, Arizona, Colorado, Pennsylvania, Virginia, Florida, and several Midwest states. Automobile insurance, a small segment of the business, is available only in Indiana.

Most policyholders neither smoke nor drink, and they are accorded better rates because of their abstinence. The company, Steiner explains, attempts "to find ways we can pay for a loss . . . our attitude is 'let's see if there is some way we can help'; if it's a borderline thing, we try to decide to the benefit of the policyholder. That's part of the thread that runs through our history."

The company's first home office was in the post office in the small

Paul A. Steiner has been president of Brotherhood Mutual Insurance Company since 1971 and chairman of the board since 1974.

Brotherhood Mutual Insurance Company occupies this ultramodern building at 6400 Brotherhood Way on the north side of Fort Wayne.

town of Grabill, Indiana, near Fort Wayne. Today some 100 employees and officers work in ultramodern corporate offices on the north side of Fort Wayne. One of the fringe benefits is unique: weekly, employee-conducted devotional services in the company auditorium. The firm also pays for insurance courses to maintain a high level of employee expertise in all facets of the business.

Brotherhood Mutual, which has 550 agents, would consider its typical clients to be church members, nonsmokers, and responsible. "There is always a lot of trust involved" in the company-client relationship, Steiner says.

The organization was founded by Albert Neuenschwander and his pastor as the Brotherhood Aid Association. Every policy issued since 1917 has carried the Bible verse from Galatians, "Bear ye one another's burdens and so fulfill the law of Christ."

In 1935 the State of Indiana declared "Brotherhood Aid" incorporate, so the name was changed to Brotherhood Mutual Insurance Company. The firm also became independent of any church affiliation to serve a broader market.

Offices were moved in 1940 to

West Wayne and Broadway, and three subsequent moves occurred before the firm relocated in 1980 to the newly constructed, 45,000-square-foot facilities occupied today at 6400 Brotherhood Way along I-69.

The firm's 71-year history was marked by a significant challenge in 1965, when three separate areas of Indiana were extensively damaged by tornadoes. The company, principal insurer in these areas, took pride in meeting its obligations to policyholders.

Paul Steiner, employed by the Brotherhood Mutual Insurance Company for 23 years, became president in 1971 and also chairman of the board three years later. In February 1988 he reported premium income during 1987 grew by 7.8 percent to $29.8 million, and the firm has an "A" (excellent) rating from A.M. Best. A man who loves the "challenge of insurance," Steiner finds pleasure in working with employees and agents to provide for the insurance needs of their clients with excellent coverages and superior service at reasonable rates.

LINCOLN NATIONAL BANK AND TRUST COMPANY

A bank whose original name reflected Fort Wayne's strong German heritage continues to prosper today in its 83rd year of operation in the city. Lincoln National Bank and Trust Company—known as the German-American National Bank when founded in 1905—was destined to more than fulfill its founders' then-novel idea: to provide services from within one bank to both business and individuals. Until then banks served either commercial or individual needs.

The bank, whose parent company was to become Lincoln Financial Corporation, the fourth-largest bank holding company based in Indiana, quickly won the hearts of both business and individual customers. The first day of business on May 20, 1905, produced 800 accounts totaling more than $100,000. Total liabilities and resources of the bank amounted to $218,960. Eighty-three years later assets totaled more than $1.7 billion.

When founders Samuel Foster and Theodore Wentz organized what was then the city's ninth bank and its fifth national banking institution, its offices were located on Court Street in downtown Fort Wayne. In April 1912, when the city's population numbered approximately 64,000 residents, the institution opened a branch office at Calhoun and Brackenridge. Stockholders organized the Lincoln Trust Company in 1914. Four years later, spurred by anti-German attitudes related to the United States' involvement in World War I, the name was changed to Lincoln National Bank. The institution absorbed the trust company and formed Lincoln National Bank and Trust Company in 1928.

Charles Buesching, who as a teenager had been employed by the bank as a messenger, became president of the institution in January 1929. The following October marked not only the catastrophic stock market collapse but also a more positive event in Fort Wayne—the start of construction of the 312-foot, art-deco Lincoln Bank Tower at 116 East Berry Street, within one block of the original bank offices.

Lincoln National Bank did better than survive an epidemic of bank failures in 1933; it became northern Indiana's largest bank of the era.

Lincoln, which today has 15 banking centers in Allen County, not only originated the branch office concept in Fort Wayne, but also for a brief period in the early 1930s sponsored two affiliate banks: North Side State Bank at 1615 Wells Street, and East Side State Bank at 1201 Maumee Avenue. Another new concept—drive-up banking—was initiated by Lincoln in the 1950s. The institution also established the area's first automated banking machine.

Robert J. DeLaney, Jr., today serves as chairman, president, and chief executive officer of the full-service institution, which is the lead bank of Lincoln Financial Corporation. In January 1988 the corporation had more than 5.6 million shares of stock outstanding and reported a total shareholders' equity of approximately $116 million.

From its grand opening in 1930 through 1970, the stately Lincoln National Bank Tower was the tallest building in Indiana. Today Lincoln National Bank has 15 banking centers in Allen County.

INDIANA MICHIGAN POWER

Significant milestones in Fort Wayne history can be traced to companies that ultimately evolved into what is today known as Indiana Michigan Power.

Some older residents still can recall with fondness the electric-powered trolleys that carried them to and from amusements at Robison Park more than 80 years ago. Electricity and the companies producing it were instrumental in hosting, in Fort Wayne, the first night baseball game in the nation, played in June 1883. The all-electric 26-story One Summit Square is a Fort Wayne landmark, built in collaboration between Summit Bank and Indiana & Michigan Electric Company (I&M), the latter recently renamed Indiana Michigan Power.

Indiana Michigan Power corporate offices are in One Summit Square, where officers and managers take obvious pride in being part of a company that has played a major role in Fort Wayne's history and development. The supplier of electricity for the city is a member of the seven-state American Electric Power system, which encompasses eight operating companies.

Three mergers stand out among many involving several small companies engaged in hydroelectric power installations and interurban streetcar enterprises. The present organization has grown out of mergers with Indiana General Service Company, which included divisions in Marion and Muncie, Indiana; Indiana and Michigan Electric Company, whose service area covered South Bend, Indiana, and St. Joseph, Michigan, divisions; and Indiana Service Corporation (ISC), which served the Fort Wayne area. The latter, and final, merger occurred in 1948, some 26 years after I&M was purchased by American Gas & Electric Company, predecessor of American Electric Power Company.

ISC, a utility company, also operated Fort Wayne's streetcars and an extensive interurban system; its roots can be traced to 1883 and a predecessor organization, Jenney Electric Light and Power Company, which promoted the night baseball game. When the merger with I&M occurred in 1948, the I&M name prevailed, and company headquarters were established at the former ISC offices at 2101 Spy Run Avenue in Fort Wayne.

An investor-owned utility, the firm now known as Indiana Michigan Power has four generating divisions, which have the combined capability of producing more than 6 million kilowatts of power.

The firm serves some 455,000 customers in 25 counties in northern and east-central Indiana and three southwestern Michigan counties, a service area encompassing 7,740 square miles and a population of 1.6 million people. Approximately 35,000 customers were added in 1974, when I&M and the City of Fort Wayne signed a 35-year lease calling for I&M to lease City Light facilities and assume service to the latter's customers.

The Indiana Michigan Power and American Electric Power transmission network comprises more than 2,000 miles of 765,000-volt lines, making it the most flexible and reliable power-delivery system ever constructed.

The 26-story, all-electric One Summit Square houses the corporate offices of Indiana Michigan Power.

The turn of the century saw such wondrous inventions as the electric-powered Fort Wayne Consolidated Railway cars pictured here (below right).

To sustain the electric supply in the area, Indiana & Michigan Electric Company sent line crews in the company-owned vehicle (below). Photo circa 1914

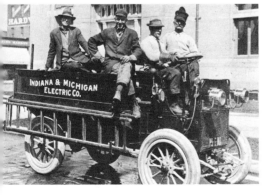

THE LUTHERAN HOSPITAL OF FORT WAYNE, INC.

The 25-bed Lutheran Hospital was purchased for $10,000 from Judge Lindley M. Ninde and formally opened on November 24, 1904.

History seems always to be in the making at the Lutheran Hospital of Fort Wayne, an organization that has been an integral part of the city since 1903, when the Lutheran Hospital Association was formally organized under the leadership of the Reverend Philipp Wambsganss.

Founders of the original hospital, a remodeled 21-room farmhouse on Fairfield Avenue, would be startled to see the dramatic changes in facilities and services that grew out of the simple beginning. Today, with more than 2,000 employees, Lutheran Hospital is one of the city's major employers and part of the largest business in the community, the health care industry.

Patient beds have grown from the original 25 in 1904 to 420. Expansions, which began as early as 1905,

have resulted in the hospital's becoming a major complex on the city's south side. Encompassing and extending far beyond the original site, it serves residents within a 75-mile radius of the hospital, in northern Indiana, southern Michigan, and northwestern Ohio.

The hospital today is the base for the Northern Indiana Heart Institute. Numerous heart transplantations have been performed at the hospital, and surgeons, in September 1987, performed the state's second artificial heart transplantation. The hospital, which established the first renal dialysis unit in Indiana, is extending outpatient services to kidney patients through freestanding facilities in Marion and Warsaw, Indiana.

These and other contemplated

achievements, including the development of the Lutheran Medical Park on a 100-acre site at I-69 and U.S. 24 in the rapidly growing southwest sector of Allen County, carry out the philosophy that motivated the early founders—A Christian Commitment to Care.

Lutherans in 1878 bought property for a hospital in the Village of South Wayne, two blocks south of the current location, but they later sold the lots to benefit Fort Wayne City Hospital, renamed Hope Hospital in 1891, at East Washington Boulevard and Barr Street in downtown Fort Wayne. However, when Hope needed to enlarge, the Lutherans decided to build their new hospital and formed a tentative association with the Reverend Philipp Wambsganss as director. He and others from Lutheran congregations were part of the formal organization of the Lutheran Hospital Association of Fort Wayne on May 11, 1903.

The Ninde homestead was purchased, remodeled, and furnished for $19,617. The building was ready by Thanksgiving 1904 and consisted of 25 patient beds, operating room, reception room, kitchen, dining room, room for the matron and her daughter, and room for an intern. Three months later the association borrowed $60,000 to expand the hospital to 75 rooms, with the addition dedicated on August 25, 1906. Nurses were housed in the original building until 1913, when the home of Judge S.R. Alden was purchased for $15,000 for this purpose.

Additional expansions came in the mid-1920s. A new wing on Wildwood Avenue afforded space for a modern obstetrics department, two delivery rooms, nursery, kitchen, and four dining rooms, and adult bed capacity grew to 215. In 1953 a $3-million project replaced the original building and added 105 beds. Dedicated in April 1956, the hospital now encompassed a new pharmacy, physiotherapy department, nine operating rooms, fracture room, cystoscopic room, post-anesthesia recovery room, new kitchen, and Chapel of Mercy. An addition of beds in 1957 brought the capacity to 385.

Numerous expansions in subsequent years saw the hospital grow to nine stories with additional wings and remodeled emergency facilities. New equipment, such as a CT full-body scanner and linear accelerator for cancer treatment, reflected modern technological advances. An intensive-care/intermediate-care nursery, and services and facilities

for high-risk premature babies also were added. The hospital continues to participate in residency programs for orthopedic surgery and family practice while supporting clinical training for medical programs and several technical programs, including medical, surgical, and radiology.

The most recent plans for Lutheran Hospital were announced in August 1987. President Frederick H. Kerr said the first phase of a new Lutheran Medical Park at I-69 and U.S. 24 will include a medical office building with facilities for outpatient services, including ambulatory surgery. The facilities are scheduled to open in October 1988. Ground is expected to be broken the following year for construction of an acute-care hospital; the site also is expected to include a nursing home, an intermediate-care facility, and apartments for senior citizens.

The original hospital site will continue to be utilized to house and expand facilities of the Lutheran College of Health Professions, which now encompasses the original School of Nursing. The Fairfield site

The Reverend Philipp Wambsganss served as chairman of the board of control and president of the board of directors of the Lutheran Hospital for 30 years until his death in 1933.

will also continue to accommodate psychiatric, chemical dependency, and rehabilitation programs.

Carl W. Moellering, chairman of the board of directors that represents area Lutheran congregations, said these plans have been under way for 10 years. Regarding the new site, he said, "We seek to carry out the mission of our hospital—namely, to provide the best medical care possible as an assist and outreach of Christ's love and as an extension of his healing ministry, so necessary and vital today. We must not forget that it is to God's glory alone that we develop and build the Lutheran Medical Park."

At the end of 1987 Lutheran Hospital counted among its major resources the 465 physicians who have medical privileges at the hospital and its several hundred adult and junior volunteers, whose hours of service totaled more than 33,016.

ZOLLNER CORPORATION

A corporation whose name has become well known in both industrial and sports worlds celebrated its 75th year of operation in 1987, in Fort Wayne, its headquarters since 1931.

The Zollner Corporation story reflects close family ties and the integrity and business acumen shared by founder and father Theodore Zollner, and his son, Fred. The high standards that have contributed to corporate progress evolved from their own expertise in manufacturing and designing aluminum pistons for leading engine manufacturers in the automotive, agricultural, and construction fields.

The Zollner story began in Duluth, Minnesota, where in 1912 Theodore Zollner, at 34 years of age, started his own business. In 1914 his son, Fred, became an apprentice in his father's business, working days and studying nights to earn a mechanical engineering degree from the University of Minnesota. By 1928 the Zollner Machine Works was widely recognized for the quality of its workmanship and its innovation in developing an aluminum piston for truck and bus engines.

In 1931 the Zollners decided to move to Fort Wayne in order to be

The Zollner Corporation was founded by Theodore Zollner in 1912. His son Fred joined him two years later as an apprentice. The company moved to Fort Wayne in 1931 to be closer to the engine manufacturers who purchased its aluminum pistons.

closer to leading engine manufacturers. When the firm moved into a new building at a site near the International Harvester plant on Fort Wayne's east side, it began operations with the 16 employees who moved with the company from Duluth.

The company expanded during World War II, producing aircraft, military truck, and tank pistons. After the war Zollner became the major independent heavy-duty piston supplier in the United States.

Zollner Corporation became known also for its community involvement in blood-donation programs, its men's chorus, and a Knot Hole Gang program, organized by Fred Zollner, which attracted more than 30,000 youngsters into various athletic activities.

Throughout the 1940s and 1950s the Zollner Pistons basketball and softball teams gained national recognition and awards; in 1947 the softball team won its third national title.

When the team disbanded in 1954, its record was 1,253 wins and 189 losses.

The Pistons basketball team also fared well during the 1940s, winning three World Professional Basketball tournaments. In 1957 the team moved to Detroit, and Fred Zollner sold the franchise in 1974. The stadium was sold in 1958 to Concordia Lutheran High School, and adjacent land was donated to Concordia and Indiana Vocational Technical College.

With expansion of physical facilities, including an automated permanent mold foundry, to 650,000 square feet at its original site, the Zollner Corporation expanded its piston sales to Ford and GM light truck gasoline engines. Sales offices are located in Chicago and Detroit, and there is a plant in Leamington, Ontario. Fred Zollner, who assumed leadership of the firm when his father died in 1952, was succeeded at his death in 1982 by Marjorie Bowstrom, chairman of the board and chief executive officer. The firm currently employs more than 1,100 people.

Marjorie Bowstrom, chairman of the board and chief executive officer, succeeded Fred Zollner, who had managed the business for 30 years until his death in 1982. The company has continued to develop and manufacture quality pistons for more than 75 years.

SUMMIT BANK

Summit Bank, with assets of more than $1.9 billion, making it Indiana's fourth-largest bank among 354, evolved from the merger in December 1983 of Peoples Trust Bank and Indiana Bank and Trust Company. In April 1987 Anthony Wayne Bank, another longtime banking institution in Fort Wayne, merged with Summit.

Summit Bank is the lead institution of Summcorp, a multibank holding company. Summit Bank assumed a rich history through the institutions it encompasses. Each has roots deeply entrenched in twentieth-century banking history in Fort Wayne.

Donnelly P. McDonald, Jr., senior vice-chairman of Summcorp and Summit Bank, is the grandson of Patrick J. "P.J." McDonald, the first secretary/treasurer and later president of the Peoples Trust and Savings Company, founded in 1903 through the leadership of attorneys William P. Breen and John Morris, Jr. P.J.'s son, Donnelly P. McDonald, Sr., became president of Peoples during the 1940s, succeeded in that office by his son, Donnelly P. McDonald, Jr., in 1961. It was in that era that the bank's name was changed to Peoples Trust Bank, and its savings and retail banking emphasis was expanded to include commercial and corporate clients. Under McDonald's leadership, the bank in the late 1970s developed plans, in collaboration with Indiana & Michigan Electric Company, for construction of the 26-story One Summit Square, which today serves as headquarters for Summcorp and Summit Bank.

Richard T. Doermer, chairman of the board and chief executive officer of Summcorp and Summit Bank, has ties to Indiana Bank and Trust, founded in Fort Wayne in 1923 by attorney Harry J. Hogan as Dime Savings and Trust Company. Doermer became president shortly after the bank changed hands in 1956. The institution was renamed Indiana Bank and Trust Company in 1958 because "the 10-cent dime isn't exactly what it used to be." When the bank merged with Peoples, it moved to One Summit Square. Anthony Wayne Bank, headed by Jay R. Powell, evolved from the Fort Wayne Morris Plan, which was established in 1915.

Today Summcorp has 8,000 shareholders in 29 states and will have access to more than 3 million—58 percent—Indiana residents upon a scheduled change in Indiana banking law in January 1989. Its holdings encompass Summit Bank, Fort Wayne, of which Darrell L. Blanton is president and chief operating officer; Summit Bank Of Marion; Summit Bank Of Clinton County in Frankfort; Summit Bank Of Kendallville; Summit Bank Of South Bend; Summit Bank Of Johnson County (south Indianapolis); Summit Bank Of Hamilton County (north Indianapolis); and Industrial Trust and Savings Bank, Muncie. Summcorp has 46 offices through its eight subsidiary banks, which offer commercial, consumer, mortgage banking, trust, investment, casualty insurance, and discount brokerage services. Summcorp is scheduled to merge with Trustcorp, a Toledo-based bank holding company, in June 1988.

The 26-story One Summit Square, shown here, was developed by Summit Bank together with Indiana & Michigan Electric Company in the late 1970s. It is headquarters for Summit Bank and its holding company, Summcorp.

PHELPS DODGE MAGNET WIRE COMPANY

Phelps Dodge Magnet Wire Company—one of the world's largest manufacturers of magnet wire—began as Inca Manufacturing Company in 1929 in the original building of the present Fort Wayne Inca magnet wire plant at 4300 New Haven Avenue. It traces its roots from the founder of the former Dudlo Manufacturing Company (1910 to 1927), the firm that established Fort Wayne as the magnet wire manufacturing center of the United States. Inca Manufacturing became part of the Phelps Dodge organization in 1931.

In 1967 Phelps Dodge built another magnet wire plant in Hopkinsville, Kentucky, which at that time more than doubled the division's physical size. Both the Inca plant and the Hopkinsville plant have been expanded considerably since they were opened. Another plant, in Elizabeth, New Jersey, came under the Phelps Dodge Magnet Wire Company banner in early 1987. Fort Wayne remains the headquarters for the organization, with executive offices at 1302 East Creighton Avenue.

Phelps Dodge Magnet Wire Company primarily manufactures and sells a full line of round, square, and rectangular film- and fabric-insulated copper and aluminum magnet wires, many of which were developed by its research and devel-

Known as Inca Manufacturing company when it was founded in 1929, the company's familiar jagged roof line and multiple exhaust stacks were its trademark. Just two years later it became an important part of the Phelps Dodge Magnet Wire Company.

opment group. It has been estimated that about half of the major magnet wire developments in commercial use today originated at Phelps Dodge. The firm holds many patents on magnet wires, enamels, and equipment.

Magnet wire is used for the windings or coils in many electrical and electronic devices. In a motor, the current in magnet wire windings creates the magnetic field that causes the motor to rotate. In residential transformers, the windings lower line voltage to the 115/220 volts standard in home use. Appliances, television sets, and automobile electrical systems depend on magnet wire to function.

Phelps Dodge Magnet Wire Company is a division of Phelps Dodge Corporation, the largest producer of copper in the United States, turning out more than one billion pounds of copper yearly from three operating domestic mines. In addition to its copper mines, Phelps Dodge and its subsidiary companies domestically operate a copper refinery, copper-fabricating mills and plants, and research and development centers. The corporation also is the world's second-largest producer of carbon black, with manufacturing facilities worldwide. In addition, Phelps Dodge Corporation participates in numerous overseas copper production facilities, mining interests, and gold and copper exploration activities.

Still at the same location, the Phelps Dodge Magnet Wire Company has expanded through its research and development programs. The firm holds many patents on magnet wires, enamels, and equipment.

TOKHEIM CORPORATION

When the owner of an Iowa hardware store and well-pump business developed an improved method for dispensing gasoline and kerosene in 1898, little did he realize he was planting the roots for what was to become an internationally recognized corporation.

John J. Tokheim, whose name in Norwegian means "take home," formed the Tokheim Manufacturing Company in 1901 to produce what was called the Tokheim Dome Oil Pump. Five years later he designed a pump with a visible measuring device, destined to become closely allied to the automotive industry. Subsequent refinements of the pump led to sales of thousands of models in the ensuing years.

In 1918 the company was sold to Ralph F. Diserens of Fort Wayne and some colleagues. All shared financial commitment to the firm they were acquiring with authorized capital stock of 200,000 shares, as well as faith in the future of the automobile industry and the related need for improved gasoline- and oil-dispensing equipment.

The Tokheim inventory was to

One of the products researched and developed is the Tokheim Convenience Systems (TCS). Sophisticated electronic timers, meters, and money-acceptance systems are only a part of the progress made in the industry after the original pump concept, developed by John J. Tokheim.

The new world headquarters of the Tokheim Corporation.

be relocated to facilities in Fort Wayne that had once housed the Wayne Spoke and Bending Company on the city's east side near the Wabash Railroad tracks. There, shareholders labored nights and weekends to restore life to the abandoned brick buildings that were to become the home of the new Tokheim Oil Tank and Pump Company.

Although most of the inventory shipped from Cedar Rapids, Iowa, was ultimately discarded, a carload of parts was utilized to create a long-distance curb pump, a product whose popularity contributed to the company becoming a major force in the gasoline pump industry within two years.

Physical facilities expanded; a sales office opened in San Francisco in 1923, the first of 24 such offices later located throughout the United States. Tokheim attracted and utilized the creative talents of many individuals to design and manufacture a variety of products, including the first electrically powered gasoline pump—the firm's first mass-produced pump—underground storage tanks, and the first gasoline pump whose bell marked each gallon of fuel delivery. More than 10,000

of these popular pumps were sold.

The firm continued to be a leader in the field through the design of innovative products. In 1952 the submerged pump was regarded as one of the most significant achievements in service station history. In 1953 its name was changed to Tokheim Corporation.

Tokheim's continuing strength hinges on its diversification efforts. Its products include electronic timers, money-acceptance systems, automotive fuel pumps, meters, a modular electronic petroleum marketing system, and other retail automation systems. Net sales in 1986 exceeded $157 million and reached nearly $200 million in 1987.

The company has plants in Fort Wayne, Albion, Fremont, and Washington, Indiana; West Chicago, Illinois; Lansdale, Pennsylvania; and Jasper and Newbern, Tennessee. International facilities are in Canada, the Netherlands, Scotland, South Africa, Germany, and Denmark. John E. Overmyer is chairman of the board and president of Tokheim Corporation.

ESSEX GROUP, INC.

Nestled in one of Fort Wayne's older neighborhoods is a firm that, since 1936, has become one of the world's foremost manufacturers of electrical wire and cable products.

Today, as in years past, homes with spacious verandas and grape arbors rub elbows with the Essex Group, Inc., a company whose extensive manufacturing facilities span across the United States. Among those facilities is the area where the original brick building initially housed 50 employees and in yet earlier years served as home for a thriving wire mill operated by Dudlo Manufacturing Company.

Early Essex history is linked to prominent Fort Wayne residents, well-known firms such as Ford Motor Company, and other Indiana businesses whose acquired facilities and/or products contributed significantly to the growth of Essex.

Essex Wire Corporation was orga-

Essex Group is one of the world's leading producers of electrical wire and cable. The company manufactures such products as magnet wire, telecommunication wire, building wire, wire for the automotive and appliance markets, and electrical insulating materials.

nized in Detroit in 1930. The firm's eventual move to Fort Wayne can be traced to W.E. Mossman, a prominent Fort Wayne resident who wanted his daughter and son-in-law to move to Fort Wayne to join the rest of the family.

Mossman's son-in-law, George Jacobs, was associated with the Sherwin-Williams Paint Company in Cleveland, Ohio. Jacobs devised the first practical enamel for coating fine wire, making it possible by 1910 to

This building on Wall Street housed Dudlo Manufacturing Company, where 50 employees operated the original wire mill. It is now part of the Essex Group's headquarters and has since been remodeled.

produce the first small-gauge magnet wire. In 1911 Jacobs, his father-in-law, and his brother-in-law, B. Paul Mossman, formed a partnership, naming their Dudlo Manufacturing Company after Jacobs' hometown of Dudley, Massachusetts.

To entice Jacobs to move his plant from rented quarters in Cleveland to Fort Wayne, W.E. Mossman built a small structure on Wall Street, and in 1912 Dudlo—and the Jacobs family—moved to Fort Wayne. The firm became a major supplier of coils for Henry Ford's Model-T automobile ignitions and a major producer of magnet wire.

In 1930 Ford concluded an agreement with Addison E. Holton in which Holton's newly incorporated firm, the Essex Wire Corporation, would produce automotive wire for the car manufacturer in a plant near Detroit. Dudlo, purchased in 1927 by General Cable Corporation, closed its doors in Fort Wayne in 1933.

Holton's firm continued acquir-

ing manufacturing companies, including RMB Manufacturing of Logansport, Indiana; Chicago Transformer Company; and Indiana Rubber and Insulated Wire Company. In 1936 Holton discovered the idle Dudlo plant in Fort Wayne. The facilities were suitable for what he had been seeking in order to accommodate growing demands for magnet wire from electric motor manufacturers. Holton acquired the Dudlo plant and equipment, and eventually Essex occupied the entire plant located at Phenie and Wall streets.

Once operations began in Fort Wayne, the Essex product line expanded to include coils, general-purpose wire, complete electrical wire assemblies, small transformers, and power cords for manufacturers of electrical equipment. Essex had 12 plants by the early 1940s. The firm was a major producer of magnet wire and lead wire for electrical motors and transformers, automotive electrical systems, and building wire and cable. In addition, World War II prompted a need for wire assemblies for B-24 bombers, field wire for the U.S. Army Signal Corps, communications equipment transformers, and wire and cable for other defense and priority domestic purposes.

The postwar era brought an increased demand for products related to electric appliances. In the 1950s expansion of the automotive industry as well as the demand for electrical insulating materials and electrical and electromagnetic controls and systems brought significant prosperity to the firm.

Holton served as president of Essex until 1959, when he was succeeded by Walter Probst. While Holton continued to serve as chairman and chief executive officer, Probst initiated organizational and consolidation measures that contributed to the firm's continuing devel-

opment. Fort Wayne became the corporate headquarters for Essex, with offices near the still-functioning plant originally occupied by the Dudlo operation.

With Holton's retirement in 1962, Probst was elected chairman and chief executive officer. The firm became a publicly held corporation in 1965, and shares were listed on the New York Stock Exchange.

Probst continued serving as chairman and chief executive officer when Paul W. O'Malley was elected president in 1966. Diversification accelerated under O'Malley's leadership, new plants were established in the United States and abroad, and the firm's name was changed to Essex International, Inc. By 1974 more than 100 plants were located in 17 states and four foreign countries, and 28,000 people were employed in 10 divisions.

A friendly merger with United Aircraft Corporation (later United Technologies Corporation) occurred in February 1974, and Essex became a wholly owned subsidiary. Probst retired later that year, and O'Malley became chairman and chief executive. Two years later the company changed its name to Essex Group, Inc. In 1978 Peter L. Scott succeeded O'Malley as president and chief executive of Essex; Probst and O'Malley continued to serve as members of

the United Technologies Corporation (UTC) board of directors.

Scott was named head of UTC's newly formed electronics group as UTC executive vice-president in 1979. James A. O'Connor, affiliated with Essex since 1949, succeeded Scott as president of Essex Group in December 1979. On January 4, 1984, John M. Bruce, former president of the Automotive Products Division of UTC Automotive, was named president of Essex Group; he was named chief executive in August 1984 and chairman in January 1985.

On February 29, 1988, Essex Group, Inc., was acquired by MS/Essex Holdings, Inc., a newly formed corporation consisting of The Morgan Stanley Leveraged Equity Fund II, L.P., members of Essex Management, and other investors.

Headquartered in Fort Wayne, Essex Group, Inc., today continues its 57-year heritage of leadership and product quality as it supplies magnet wires, electrical wires, and cables to the automotive, appliance, construction, electrical equipment, and telecommunications industries.

In 1930 Essex Wire Corporation began constructing automotive wire harnesses in a leased corner of Ford Motor Company's Highland Park factory. By the 1970s every U.S.-built car included at least one Essex product.

GREATER FORT WAYNE CHAMBER OF COMMERCE

The late 1980s find the Greater Fort Wayne Chamber of Commerce actively involved in the community it has served for 113 years.

Enthusiastically promoting economic development for Fort Wayne, which earlier in the decade was recognized nationally as "Most Livable City" and "All America City," the chamber of commerce in 1987 undertook a vigorous member-recruitment effort that attracted more than 620 new member busi-

nesses. It currently serves more than 2,000 business and industrial member firms.

Earlier in this decade the chamber helped restore some 25,000 jobs lost to the city in the early 1980s, some 10,000 of these due to International Harvester's leaving Fort Wayne. The organization also was involved in successful efforts to lure General Motors to the area and, more recently, took an active role in inducing the Detroit-based Cadillac Coffee Company to choose Fort Wayne in an expansion move calling for the firm to invest some $2.2 million in new facilities.

In 1983, during the presidency of Richard G. Clark, a chamber fund drive raised $9.2 million, a record for any local chamber of commerce in the nation. Under James Dittoe, who succeeded Clark as president in Feb-

ruary 1986, the chamber is focusing particular attention on economic activity and expansion of business, promotion of downtown development, improvement of transportation services and facilities, and development of export markets. Some $200,000 has been allocated to the Japan Development Project, a two-year venture through which the chamber hopes to attract at least six Japanese companies and 600 new jobs to Fort Wayne by late 1988. By their nature, chambers of commerce look to the present and future more than the past, yet a look backward is inevitable as the organization moves into its 113th year of operation in 1988.

A small group of young men has been credited with organizing the city's first chamber of commerce in 1875; during the tenure of the first president, John M. Coombs, some 70 businessmen became members. In 1910 the organization formally named the chamber of commerce grew out of a merger of the Fort Wayne Commercial Club and the Wayne Club.

The attractive brick building still occupied by the chamber at the corner of Ewing and West Wayne streets was constructed in 1926 at a cost of $350,000. The venture grew out of a gift of $10,000 by Louis Fox and an additional fund-raising effort.

The Greater Fort Wayne Chamber of Commerce has occupied this building at the corner of Ewing and West Wayne streets since 1926. Extensive interior remodeling has taken place through the years (above).

A breakfast seminar is held in one of the chamber's rooms. Encouraging industry to relocate to the Fort Wayne area is one of the major concerns of the chamber (left).

At the same time the Fort Wayne Women's Bureau contributed financially to the project to provide rooms for its programs; the organization continues to utilize the building's third floor today.

Interior remodeling projects were undertaken in 1964; during Clark's tenure, from 1982 to 1985, a more extensive modernization project was completed, and the longtime restaurant service was discontinued.

The Greater Fort Wayne Chamber of Commerce has a current budget of $1.6 million and 20 staff members.

The original men's club room of the Greater Fort Wayne Chamber of Commerce.

INDIANA VOCATIONAL TECHNICAL COLLEGE

The Fort Wayne campus of Indiana Vocational Technical College has grown in enrollment from 130 students to approximately 3,000 since opening in the city in 1969 as one of 13 regional, state-supported vocational technical institutions created through legislation approved by the Indiana General Assembly in 1963. The legislators' primary goal was to enhance the vocational skills of post-high school students while also strengthening economic development opportunities in the state.

Initially occupying the third-floor classrooms it leased in the former Concordia High School building at Maumee Avenue and Anthony Boulevard, the College—commonly referred to as Ivy Tech—provided courses in drafting, engineering, and secretarial skills to its first 130 students. The curriculum and enrollment expanded quickly and dramatically. Today students, who are drawn from nine northeastern Indiana counties served by the regional College, have a choice of 27 programs.

Most classes are offered at its campus situated since 1976 at North Anthony Boulevard and Coliseum Boulevard East on land deeded to

Approximately 50 percent of the students of Indiana Vocational Technical College are from Fort Wayne. Shown here are industrial maintenance students learning to use the latest programmable controllers.

Ivy Tech by Indiana University and donated by the Zollner Corporation. Part of its 80,000-square-foot facility there was constructed by the Northeast Indiana Construction Advancement Foundation. The College also utilizes leased classroom space at the Fort Wayne State Developmental Center and at the new Concordia High School near the College campus.

Some of the programs added since 1969 reflect employer needs within the region: robotics, CAD, statistical process control, fire science, culinary arts, child care, practical nursing, information/data management, and building construction technology. The College periodically adapts its curriculum to meet economic and job development needs within the region.

The average student at the Fort Wayne campus today is about 28 years old (many are younger and some are considerably older). Along with recent high school graduates are a significant number who have bachelor's degrees or years of work experience, and attend the College to update and/or prepare for career changes. At least 50 percent are from Fort Wayne.

Administration of the statewide system is through a 13-member board of trustees appointed by the governor and a president named by this board. Each of the 13 regions is governed by its own seven-member

Known as Ivy Tech, the institution has a current enrollment of about 3,000 students. Word processing, another highly technical skill that is needed in modern-day business, is taught at the school.

board of trustees, also appointed by the state board. Mearle R. Donica was the first regional director in Fort Wayne; the position now carries the title of vice-president/dean, an office held since 1982 by Jon L. Rupright.

Ivy Tech College has been accredited since 1977 by the Commission on Institutions of Higher Education of the North Central Association of Colleges and Schools. Full-time faculty members are assisted by a part-time staff of trained professionals who are actively employed in their fields. Depending upon the program completed, students receive a one-year technical certificate or a two-year Associate in Applied Science degree. The College also offers custom training for businesses and industrial firms.

FORT WAYNE DOWNTOWN HILTON

Fort Wayne's second-largest hotel—Fort Wayne Hilton at the Convention Center—is less than three years old but already is in the throes of psychological and financial "rebirth." The nine-story, 250-room $19.2- million hotel, focal point of rejuvenation in downtown Fort Wayne, was built to complement and accommodate the adjoining convention facility, Grand Wayne Center.

Opening to high praise and great expectations in late September 1985, the hotel incorporated a lavish style a now-former owner described as "eclectic traditional." Appointments and attitudes were in the manner of expensive European-style hostelries. High tea, uniformed bellhops and pageboys, doormen in top hats, management in formal attire, and Lady Godiva chocolates gracing the pillows of hotel guests were among the special touches that quickly captured the attention of the media and guests.

In May 1987 the hotel was purchased by Lincoln National Corporation, a major insurance company headquartered in Fort Wayne, and Servico, a hotel management firm of West Palm Beach, Florida.

Joseph A. Corso, a Servico employee who has 17 years' experience in hotel management, was named general manager in early 1988. He and the new owners have set about changing the hotel's previously somewhat aloof, elitist image to one of what Corso describes as "a friend, rather than an inanimate object." He explains, "I know the importance of being involved in a city. You can't be an island unto yourself. The new owners aspire to give the hotel a community image."

To accomplish this goal, Corso says, he is aided by a "very hospitable staff of 260 employees who care." The hotel will actively involve itself in community events, and Corso talks of plans, which would in-volve the hotel and other community organizations, to draw sports celebrities and events to downtown Fort Wayne.

It is not Corso's natural inclination to "sit and wait" for the public to perceive the Fort Wayne Hilton's new civic-minded personality, but he says some patience is needed and he is confident. The two-to-five-year goal, Corso says, is "to have the local residents utilize all outlets in the hotel and to financially position the hotel so that it's a profit center. It's not a thriving investment yet, but through proper ownership , employee participation, and management, it's an excellent investment."

Among the unique accommodations at the Fort Wayne Hilton is the L'Orangerie Lounge where flowering trees and plants become a natural extension of the city's Botanical Conservatory, located immediately across the street from the hotel.

PATRONS

The following individuals, companies, and organizations have made a valuable commitment to the quality of this publication. Windsor Publications and the Allen County-Fort Wayne Historical Society gratefully acknowledge their participation in *Fort Wayne Cityscapes.*

Allen County Genealogical Society of Indiana
Automation Engineering Inc.
Charles Banet, C.P.P.S.
Barr Street Irregulars
Brotherhood Mutual Insurance Company*
Carpetland USA*
Ramona Kerr Carroll
Central Soya Company, Inc.*
Coldwell Banker Banks Mallough
Cole. Mattot. Architects
Custom Research & Tabulations
Dana Corporation Spicer Axle Division*
Essex Group, Inc.*
Fort Wayne Area Home Schools
Fort Wayne Downtown Hilton*
Fort Wayne National Bank*
Greater Fort Wayne Chamber of Commerce*
Harding, Dahm & Company, Inc.
Harold H. Hawfield, M.D.
Indiana Michigan Power*
Indiana Vocational Technical College*
Irmscher Suppliers Inc.
ITT Aerospace/Optical Division*

Klaehn Funeral Homes
LightWorld, Inc. DBA LightWorld/Fans Plus
Lincoln Foodservice Products, Inc.*
Lincoln National Bank and Trust Company*
Mr. & Mrs. Duane E. Lupke
The Lutheran Hospital of Fort Wayne, Inc.*
Magnavox Government and Industrial Electronics Company
The News-Sentinel
North American Van Lines*
Jerry D. Nuerge
O'Rourke, Andrews & Maroney, Inc.
Phelps Dodge Magnet Wire Company*
Professional Federal Credit Union
Pulitzer Broadcasting Company
The Schenkel Corporation
Settlers, Inc.
Snelling and Snelling
Summit Bank*
Summit Bank Newcomer Center
Mrs. Wayne L. Thieme
Tokheim Corporation*
Alen & Anne Wyss
Zollner Corporation*

*Partners in Progress of *Fort Wayne Cityscapes.* The histories of these companies and organizations appear in Chapter 6, beginning on page 99.

SELECTED BIBLIOGRAPHY

In addition to the secondary sources listed below, numerous articles in the *Old Fort News,* the Fort Wayne Historical Society's quarterly magazine of history, and several articles published in the *Indiana Magazine of History* proved invaluable in researching *Fort Wayne Cityscapes.*

Ankenbruck, John. *Five Forts.* Fort Wayne, Ind.: Lion's Head Publishing Co., 1972.

-------. *The Fort Wayne Story.* Northridge, Calif.: Windsor Publications, 1980.

-------. *Twentieth-Century History of Fort Wayne, Indiana.* Fort Wayne, Ind.: Twentieth-Century Historical Fort Wayne, Inc., 1976.

-------. *Voice of the Turtle.* Fort Wayne, Ind.: The News Publishing Co., 1974.

Anson, Bert. *The Miami Indians.* Norman, Okla.: The University of Oklahoma Press, 1970.

Bradley, George. *Fort Wayne and Wabash Valley Trolleys.* Detroit: Central Electric Railfans' Association, 1983.

-------. *Fort Wayne's Fire Department.* Fort Wayne, Ind.: Allen County-Fort Wayne Historical Society, 1964.

-------. *Fort Wayne's Trolleys.* Chicago: Owen Davies, 1963.

Brice, Wallace A. *History of Fort Wayne, Indiana.* Fort Wayne, Ind.: D.W. Jones & Son, 1868.

Fatout, Paul. *Indiana Canals.* West Lafayette, Ind.: Purdue University Press, 1972.

Griswold, Bert J. *The Builders of Greater Fort Wayne.* Fort Wayne, Ind.: The Hoosier Press, 1926.

-------. *Guide to Fort Wayne, Indiana.* Fort Wayne, Ind.: B.J. Griswold and Charles A. Phelps, 1914.

-------. *The Pictorial History of Fort Wayne, Indiana.* 2 vols. Chicago: Robert O. Law Co., 1917.

Kinietz, W. Vernon. *The Indians of the Upper Great Lakes, 1615-1760.* Ann Arbor, Mich.: University of Michigan Press, 1965.

Knapp, H.S. *History of the Maumee Valley.* Toledo, Ohio: Blade Mammoth Co., 1872.

Lindley, Harlow. *Indiana as Seen by Early Travelers.* Indianapolis: Indiana Historical Society, 1916.

McAfee, Robert. *A History of the Late War in the Western Country.* Bowling Green, Ohio: Bowling Green University Press, 1919.

McCulloch, Hugh. *Man and Measures of Half a Century.* New York: Charles Scribner's Sons, 1888.

Neely, Mark. *Easy To Remember.* Fort Wayne, Ind.: Lincoln National Life Insurance Co., 1980.

Poinsatte, Charles. *Fort Wayne during the Canal Era, 1828-1855.* Indianapolis: Indiana

Historical Society, 1969.

-------. *Outpost in the Wilderness: Fort Wayne, 1706-1828.* Fort Wayne, Ind.: Allen County-Fort Wayne Historical Society, 1976.

Quimby, George Irving. *Indian Life in the Upper Great Lakes, 11,000 B.C. to A.D. 1800.* Chicago: University of Chicago Press, 1960.

Roberts, Bessie K. *Fort Wayne's Family Album.* Fort Wayne, Ind.: Cummins Printing Co., 1960.

Robertson, Robert. *Valley of the Upper Maumee River.* 2 vols. Madison, Wis.: Brant and Fuller, 1889.

Tanner, Helen Hornbeck. *Atlas of Great Lakes Indian History.* Norman, Okla.: University of Oklahoma Press, 1986.

Terrell, W.H.H. *Indiana in the War of the Rebellion.* Indianapolis: Indiana Historical Society, 1960.

Thronbrough, Gayle. *Letter Book of the Indian Agency at Fort Wayne, 1809-1815.* Indianapolis: Indiana Historical Society, 1961.

-------. *The Negro in Indiana before the Civil War.* Indianapolis: Indiana Historical Society, 1969.

Woehrmann, Paul. *At the Headwaters of the Maumee: A History of the Forts of Fort Wayne.* Indianapolis: Indiana Historical Society, 1971.